Kyle Cooper

MONOGRAPHICS

Kyle Cooper

Andrea Codrington

Yale University Press

Published in North America by
Yale University Press
P.O. Box 209040
New Haven, CT 06520-9040

First published in Great Britain in 2003 by
Laurence King Publishing Ltd, London

Library of Congress Control Number
2003104783

ISBN 0-300-09951-7

Designed by Brad Yendle,
Design Typography, London
Series editor : Rick Poynor

Printed in China

Frontispiece: Detail of *Sphere*, 1998.
Director: Barry Levinson
Title sequence: Kyle Cooper (creative dir.)
for Imaginary Forces

Contents

Through the Glass Darkly

Kyle Cooper. Photograph by Michael Power.

Kyle Cooper is a postmodern paradox. He is an iconoclast who loves what he transgresses, whether the tenets of modernist typography, the idea of apple-pie America or even the belief in an all-loving, all-powerful God. He is by nature betwixt and between, not quite fitting into the commercial world of Hollywood and not entirely at home in the realm of high-design discourse. He is a true-believing Christian whose oeuvre has often lingered on the sinister themes of murder and madness. The work that he has created over the past decade – first at R/Greenberg and then at Imaginary Forces, the studio he cofounded in 1996 with Peter Frankfurt and Chip Houghton – distinctively plays off this tension to great effect.

In an age predicated on irony – the knowing collusion between auteur and audience via winking references made at breakneck speed – Cooper's work comes into bold relief, for it is marked by something that seems all but lost in our cleverness-as-king culture: earnestness. This may sound an odd description for a designer who first came to
36 fame with the opening titles for David Fincher's 1995 film *Seven*, a sequence characterized by degraded, hand-scrawled type and nerve-jangling imagery. But Cooper has realized something important: desecration is all the more effective when the ideals being torn down are ones that are dearly held by the desecrater.

Kyle Cooper's short-form artistry is particularly appreciated in a culture known for its collective attention deficit disorder because it delivers intense experiences in quick bursts. The fact that such jags of entertainment have snuck into the unassuming cultural spaces of legally mandated credit sequences is a testament to both the creative urge and, perhaps, consumer culture's discomfort in the presence of blank, unmediated space. Cooper himself displays a tendency toward fitful absorption – darting associatively in conversation from one topic to the next, multi-tasking to such an extent that many of the interviews that fill his dictionary-sized book of press clippings were given on his cell phone while driving the freeways of Los Angeles county. He's even been known to read scripts while walking the Rose Bowl track for hours at a time.[1]

Although he's not the first designer to take possession of this liminal creative space, Cooper is one of the most recent figures to bring it to its current narrative fever pitch – and certainly the first to garner higher praise for his titles than the films have elicited themselves. Ever since commercial films became popular in the early 20th century, credit sequences have been used in some manner to set the tone for the stories that follow. Usually, this happened in literal ways: credits played against the backdrop of billowing sails in swashbuckler adventures, or on brown-edged parchment in historical dramas. The first title sequence to animate type in a subject-appropriate way was Victor Fleming's 1939 Civil War weepy *Gone with the Wind*, which featured titles that gust on and off the screen, italicized as if by sheer gale force.

It wasn't until Saul Bass's disjointed, bebop titles for Otto Preminger's 1955 *The Man with the Golden Arm* that credit sequences became less-than-literal narrative devices – and repositories of the cultural zeitgeist. Bass used nervous jazz riffs, bold, flat graphics and *nouvelle vague* jump cuts to create an atmospheric prelude to Preminger's tale of a junkie trumpet player played by Frank Sinatra. Taking Bass's cue, designers like Pablo Ferro (*Dr. Strangelove*), Stephen Frankfurt (*To Kill a Mockingbird*) and Maurice Binder (the James Bond films) proceeded to evolve a graphic narrative form that was increasingly complementary to the film's content and evocative of the cultural atmosphere in which it was made.

If *The Man with the Golden Arm* was highly influenced by the work of jazzmen like John Coltrane, then Kyle Cooper's most primal cues come from American horror films. Growing up in a seaside town outside Boston called Swampscott in the 1960s and '70s, Cooper spent his childhood reading horror comicbooks such as *Tales from the Crypt* and magazines like *Fangoria* and *Famous Monsters of Filmland*.[2] More fascinating, to him, however, were the visual mechanics behind gruesome movies such as *The Exorcist* and *An American Werewolf in London*. Cooper buried himself in such do-it-yourself books as the seminal *Monster Make-Up Handbook* by makeup-effect artist Dick Smith, which teaches tricks of the trade like how to render the falling away of flesh in intricate detail or true-to-life throat-cut effects. Yet rather than delving deep into the horror genre, Cooper spent his time working the literal surface – trying to figure out how to build realistic sculptures

As an adolescent, Cooper pored over how-to effects books like Dick Smith's *Monster Make-Up Handbook*.

of zombies with arrows piercing their eyes. Such verisimilitude required familiarity with the body's inner workings, and Cooper also immersed himself in medical journals, studying the myriad ways in which things can go wrong.

While Cooper's youthful emphasis on replicating the physical manifestations of the horror genre has been replaced over the years by a focus on its psychic machinations, this early obsession with flayed bodies and anatomical pathologies seems to have led to a desire to tear away at the surface of things – to reveal the metaphorical blood and guts that lie just beneath the skin of reality. In the same way that Alfred Hitchcock was known to set the most dastardly plots against the backdrop of national monuments such as Mt. Rushmore (*North by Northwest*) or the Golden Gate Bridge (*Vertigo*), Cooper repeatedly picks away at American icons, in order, more often than not, to reveal something sinister.

An opening Cooper directed for John Frankenheimer's 1997 cable
66 TV film on George Wallace – the American governor of Alabama who attempted to thwart the Civil Rights movement – features close-ups of an American flag that has dark figures from historical photos superimposed on its red-and-white stripes. As the camera pans over, however, it becomes clear that these figures are in fact rents and holes in the flag, and that the red is blood-soaked cloth. The almighty dollar
26 is similarly desecrated at Cooper's hands. For *Dead Presidents*, a 1995 film directed by the Hughes Brothers about robbers hijacking an armoured car, Cooper's opening shows details of money burning: slowly, glowingly, gloriously, the faces of American presidents Benjamin Franklin and Andrew Jackson catch fire and then implode into nothingness. (Real money, it turns out, doesn't make for dramatic enough conflagrations, so Cooper and his R/Greenberg collaborators created larger-than-life replicas out of various paper stocks that proved more telegenic.) And in *Seven*, the serial killer strikes with surgical precision, excising the word "God" from the motto that appears on all American legal tender, "In God We Trust." While this may just seem like an odd, twisted detail to some, Cooper's intention was to highlight the killer's most egregious transgression. "He made himself God," says Cooper of the killer. "He became the judge of humanity."[3]

This last scene was not one that Cooper took lightly. Evil is serious business for a man whose Christian faith became zealous after his mother fell into a coma for three years and finally died, and who believes strongly in the existence of evil as an active, supernatural force in the world. To those who may find it bizarre or hypocritical for Cooper to linger on the dark, unsavoury sides of humanity, he demands, "Why deny the existence of evil? Let's all look at it for what it is." Cooper's unconventional Christian stance has, ironically, led Hollywood insiders to dub Imaginary Forces as "the evil guys".

Cooper also destabilizes that symbol of American comfort and safety, the suburbs, by contrasting quaint external appearance with queasy internal reality. The main titles for director Mark Pellington's first major feature *Arlington Road* (1999) comprise classic images of American suburbia – white picket fences, dogs, kids on bicycles and so forth – that are reversed out in negative or shot on stock that is tinted in nauseating yellows and reds. Cooper's titles, accompanied by a dissonant sound track, provide an entirely appropriate entrée into a film that takes place in a suburb of Washington, D.C., and concerns a man who is increasingly convinced that his neighbours are terrorists. In this instance, the paranoid anxiety that forms the spine of the film is set in place before a single word is spoken.

Although much of his oeuvre lingers on dark topics, Cooper claims his real fascination is with the visual complexity of nature. He remembers a time from his childhood when he spent seven weeks using a pin to draw the details of a mutant dragon's scales on a metal plate. Cooper's absorption in visual microcosms continues to this day. "It may be a faulty paradigm," he admits, "but I do respect things that are intricate. The dysfunction came from needing to create all these incredibly detailed drawings because my parents were getting divorced or my mother was in a coma – or needing to make intricate edits because I was breaking up with a girlfriend or people were taking advantage of me."

Interestingly, Cooper's description of his own creative absorption parallels that of John Doe, the serial killer in *Seven*. (Cooper confesses to putting himself in the killer's head during the shoot, even going through his own house in search of dead bugs, matted hair and all manner of "disturbing, violent, interesting things".) The killer's hands are shown carefully sewing together a book that painstakingly details both the rationale and methodology behind his plans to kill those he thinks have transgressed the Seven Deadly Sins. Doe writes prolifically, studiously clips articles from books and newspapers and collects images with a passion and rigor that most aspiring artists and writers would envy – were it not for the fact that he is pathological.

10

Cooper's darkly vivid imagination and obsession with detail are manifest in this etching from his adolescence.

Taken out of context, here is a portrait of an artist transported by inspiration, focusing all of his energies on controlling the circumstances of his inner world through the creation of an artist's book.

Despite having studied under hyper-modernist Paul Rand during graduate school at Yale University, Cooper seems in most instances to have cast aside a less-is-more approach in favour of an attention to baroque detail. The complexities of insect physiognomy come to the
68 fore in the main titles for *Mimic* (1997), a film about an entomologist's search for a cure to a deadly disease spread by cockroaches that is killing the children of Manhattan. (It goes wrong, of course, and results in an even more serious problem: killer moths that mimic the human form.) In a sequence that has all the concentrated eeriness and obsessive flourish of *Seven*, Cooper hints at the film's narrative by building in visual clues: insects pinned to a card in a researcher's vitrine, newspaper clippings decrying a modern-day plague, glassine specimen envelopes and a lower-case font that replicates all over the screen. Cooper and collaborator Karin Fong initially had a difficult time finding a creative solution for this sequence. After travelling all over Southern California to "bug shows" in search of specimens for inspiration, Cooper realized that the macro approach was the answer: "Here in this one frame, in this tiny corner, this tiny hook on the bug's leg is really wild," he suggested at the time. "Maybe we could build a storyboard about this."

Visual complexity is also at the centre of Cooper's main titles for
80 Barry Levinson's *Sphere* (1998), a tale of a large, mysterious orb on the ocean floor. In this instance, the contrast between old-fashioned etchings of wide-jawed sea monsters and the technological intricacies of rippling, spherized type induces a sense of historical and physical displacement. Deep water, like deep space, has its own alternative reality, filled with inchoate terrors and time warps – themes that are fleshed out in the film but metaphorically introduced in Cooper's eerie opening sequence.

Cooper reached the pinnacle of frenzy in his title sequence for
44 John Frankenheimer's 1996 remake of *The Island of Dr. Moreau*, which features 400 discrete shots squeezed into a little more than two-and-a-half minutes – a visually orgiastic assault on the senses that took more than four months to edit. Asked by Frankenheimer to create titles that would evoke a sense of "cellular violence" – the film is about the disastrous metamorphic results of genetic tinkering –

ABOVE AND OPPOSITE A critical part of the pre-production process occurs when the director consults with a storyboard artist. In this instance, Cooper discussed his ideas about the opening sequence of *The Island of Dr. Moreau* with favoured collaborator Wayne Coe, an illustrator and filmmaker himself, who jotted down initial visualizations involving eyes and cellular mutation.

Cooper and his RGA/LA team assembled a wildly heterogeneous array of visual source material, including stock medical photography, digital illustrations and computer-generated animation. Not only was the imagery of varying media, it was also of disparate age and quality – a fact that would have made the relentlessly aggressive sequence a near-impossibility without the help of digital technology.

The viewer first enters the title sequence through the irises of various animals, and then the rumble begins: cells collide and mutate, microscopic beasts duke it out like prize fighters, blood courses through veins with hot urgency. And all the while, the accompanying typography has its own transmorphic seizures, reproducing itself, stretching and lashing out in dangerous,

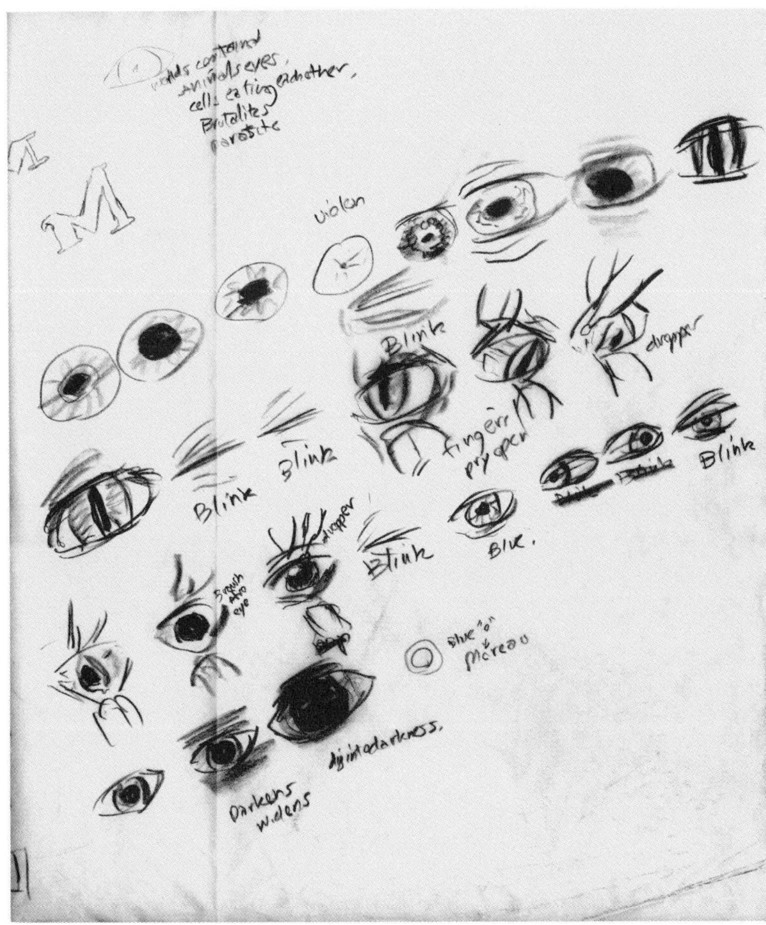

sharp-looking spikes. "We wanted the type to hurt when it hit you," Cooper once admitted of the Bembo and Mason fonts he skilfully tormented.

Cooper takes American typographer Beatrice Ward's idea of type as a "crystalline goblet" – a transparent, neutral vessel of content – and shatters it into jagged pieces.[4] He does this all the more effectively because he knows the tenets of typography from his time at Yale, and claims to hire only designers who have a particular sensitivity to type. To this day, he holds up Paul Rand as one of his greatest personal influences, the man who taught him that an idea is only as good as its execution – a rigorous benchmark that Cooper admits to be still working toward. One poster created at Yale in 1988 reflects Cooper's distinctly Randian sensitivity to type and symbolism:

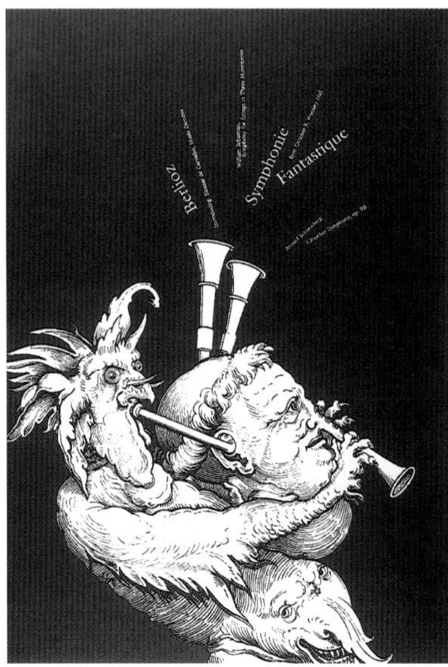

ABOVE Fond of tight type and conceptual imagery, Cooper created a series of posters for Paul Rand while a student at Yale.

RIGHT While at Yale's graduate design programme, Cooper was equally under the influence of Paul Rand and Christianity, as evidenced in this student poster.

A Call to Prayer

An invitation to all Christian students at Yale
to unite in prayer for God to manifest His power and love on our campus.
Dwight Hall, February 25, 1988 9:30 pm

For spiritual awakening
among the entire Yale community: administration, staff, faculty, and students.

For unity and cooperation among all Christian student organizations.

For revival in the hearts of all believers on campus
so that we will live unreservedly for Christ in the power of His Holy Spirit.

Sponsored by The Yale Student Chapter of Campus Crusade for Christ

Pre-Yale visual experimentations took the form of typographic method acting, which would become one of Cooper's hallmarks.

"A Call to Prayer" for all Christians on campus takes the serifs on Yale's famous blue "Y" and extends them into a crucifix.

Cooper especially treasures a presentation booklet that Rand created to pitch a redesign of the Ford logo in 1966 that is all white space, impeccable type and cleverly juxtaposed imagery – a visual sequencing that is distinctly cinematic. Rand might have been notoriously dismissive of Cooper's desire to merge design and film in his master's thesis – and even gibed that the much-heralded *Seven*
sequence was "trash art" when he finally saw it – but his insistence 15
on balanced type and image has left its mark on Cooper's work. No matter how densely layered or visually fraught his sequences appear in real time, pause on a frame and there is most likely an intentionally thought-out composition frozen on screen. "The obsessive part of me wants to have not one frame that I would second-guess," says Cooper. "I have a few pieces like that, where I could watch it 700 times and wouldn't change a thing."

Long before Cooper even knew who Paul Rand was, though, he began playing with text by taking words from the dictionary and drawing them in a way that mimicked their meaning. One experiment in 1981 had Cooper rendering the word "extort" with a gun-wielding hand as a serif on the "r" and "extinguish" with an upside-down "u" that looks like a bucket pouring out water. Without realizing it, Cooper hit upon a method that would become emblematic of his later work. In many of his title sequences, Cooper creates what could best be described as typographic method acting, wherein words animate in
54 a way that is appropriately symbolic of the film's content. In *Twister*, a film about meteorologists chasing the tornado of a lifetime, the routine names of cast and crew fly across the screen as storm-strewn debris, arrange themselves long enough to be legible, then splinter apart. For
100 *Spider-Man* (2002), Cooper has letters coalesce into names and titles that look like flies stuck in a spider's web. A similar effect occurs in
62 *Flubber* (1997), a remake of Walt Disney's '60s-era *Absent-Minded Professor* featuring mathematical notations that whizz around the screen to
90 form the credits, and *The Mummy* (1999), which draws upon Egyptian hieroglyphs and vertical as well as horizontal lettering.

It is interesting to note, however, that this sub-species of film titling usually appears in Cooper's most mainstream Hollywood jobs. As typographically clever as these may be, they are less demonstrative of Cooper's narrative vision – an indication, perhaps, of the often rigid hierarchy between film studio and title house, or what Cooper terms the "vendor mentality". Of course, the financial exigencies of running a business necessitate taking on projects that are distinctly high budget and low content. More often than not, the way the main titles and credit sequences look is an afterthought to which a fraction of production time and money is dedicated. "With main titles you have to get the names across and hopefully get people excited for the movie," notes Cooper. "Ideally it would be a stand-alone piece that would be interesting in its own right, but maybe that's self-serving."

In 1997, amidst the Imaginary Forces-led titles renaissance, the head of the Academy of Motion Picture Arts & Society responded to the question of whether film openers might be Oscar-eligible in the "Short Subjects" category with a glib "remote possibility" – an indication of how title directors tend to be ranked by the industry, no matter how spectacular their work.[5] Ironically, Cooper and his team at Imaginary Forces were chosen to create all the graphics packages for the 2002 Academy Awards, including a salute to film composers that used the show's graphic spotlight theme in a clever, Eames-reminiscent multiscreen presentation; Cooper was also commissioned
106 to create a series of stamps commemorating the craft of filmmaking.

Be that as it may, Cooper has been heralded repeatedly in mainstream magazines such as *Entertainment Weekly* – he was even voted one of the "Top 100 Most Creative People in Entertainment" in 1997 – and featured in countless design publications and competitions. Despite such recognition, he manages to assume the persona of an outsider looking in. Fittingly, the most recurrent motif in his oeuvre is the eye – wide, naked and very often a mute witness to extremes in
56 human behaviour. Eyes dominate title sequences for films like *Donnie Brasco* (1997), *The Island of Dr. Moreau* and *Mimic*, as well as in commercial spots for Sega and filmic dream sequences he has created for director
92 Julie Taymor's film production of Shakespeare's play *Titus Andronicus* (1999). Eyes activate sequences, very often by pulling the viewer through hidden Alice-in-Wonderland rabbit holes – or, as critic Janet Abrams once wrote in *I.D.*, by acting as "giant vortices sucking in one's own vision".[6]

Publicity shots of Cooper are revealing; often he highlights his eyes by covering his mouth or peeking through outspread fingers in unspoken reference to the horror genre that so impressed him as a child. As passive participants in Cooper's micro-narratives, we often see things we shouldn't – a serial killer plotting his next murders, cellular warfare – but we are like Jamie Leigh Curtis in *Halloween*'s

Wayne Coe's storyboard for *Spider-Man* shows Cooper's completed concept – a sticky tribute to the spider-and-fly relationship.

famous closet sequence, peering out between the slats, wondering what's next. Such voyeurism, of course, does not go unpunished. If eyes are a symbol of humanity, Cooper's sequences often violate, or
76 even negate, the individual. His opening for the 1998 film *Nightwatch*, for instance, features pictures of the story's victims – always teenage girls – with their eyes cut out. And in the 2001 music video for the Butthole Surfers song "Shame of Life", Cooper's nightmarish storyline includes tattooing eyeballs with red ink type.

Perhaps Cooper's familiarity with being on the outside looking in served to fuel the impeccable creative solution he directed for the
56 main titles of *Donnie Brasco*, the mob film by Mike Newell in which an FBI agent (Johnny Depp) goes under cover to infiltrate the life of a Mafioso (Al Pacino). The sequence begins with a full-on black-and-white image of Depp's dark-circled, troubled eyes looking downward. The action of the titles and the accompanying music – Beethoven's slow-moving *Pathétique* – begin the minute his eyes look up, and the rest of the sequence comprises primarily black-and-white and colour stills taken in filmstrip surveillance fashion. The credits drift on and

off in delicate white all-capped sans serifs that are oddly kerned in a subtle indication of subterfuge and imbalance. The combination results in a mood so redolent of conflict and melancholy that *New Yorker* critic Anthony Lane was moved to write in the first line of his film review, "The most beautiful thing about *Donnie Brasco* is the opening credit sequence . . . No one has had eyes like that, not since El Greco stopped painting saints."[7]

Lane's comment about Cooper's appetizer being more satisfying than the director's main course has been echoed a number of times. Lane has also written about Cooper's credits for Brian De Palma's
50 *Mission: Impossible* (1996) as being "so tense and sexy that you could leave the theater immediately afterward without suffering the letdown of the film itself."[8] And then there is Janet Maslin of the *New York Times* writing of Cooper's "rousing, majestic montage" for Rob Reiner's 1996 film about the Civil Rights movement, *Ghosts of Mississippi*. "None of what follows," she concludes, "matches the impact of this title sequence."[9]

When confronted with the view that the quality of his title sequences may well exceed that of the films themselves, Cooper is insistently modest. "That's the worst thing for me," he admitted in a 1998 interview on the web zine *Feed*. "As a graphic designer I have to solve [the director's] problem, and if I'm not listening to the director and not giving him something that works in the service of his movie that's not going to get me any work."

Too little work, it seems, is not an abiding problem for Cooper, whose Hollywood-based Imaginary Forces has grown from zero to 102 employees in less than five years. As Cooper evolves his own talent and reputation it's possible that the "vendor mentality" may become something more like competitive anxiety. (There's even one story in which a certain director was so fed up with hearing praise for Cooper in the press that he refused comments to a reporter, insisting that the article should be about his own work.) "It's a little bit difficult to work with filmmakers whose creative point of view you don't necessarily agree with," says Cooper, "especially when their direction is inconsistent with what you think is either appropriate or tasteful."

Of course, comparing the art of film-title design with long-form filmmaking presents real problems. Films take in excess of two hours to develop complex narrative arcs and three-dimensional characters. Film titles take a little over two minutes to paint a mood in a few large – or a thousand small – imagistic strokes. To penetrate these densely choreographed mini-narratives it is often necessary to splinter the surface of real time: pause, rewind and pause again to understand the contortionist constituents that go into making a seamless motion-graphics sequence. The film-title genre may present a narrative continuum, but such temporal solidity is merely an illusion born of countless hours in the editing room.

One thing that close examination reveals is that despite his reputation as master of the quick-cut "scratchy" idiom, Cooper is sensitive to editorial appropriateness. This sensitivity no doubt has its origins in Cooper's Yale studies of Sergei Eisenstein, the early 20th-century Russian filmmaker whose seminal works like *Battleship Potemkin* pioneered an entirely original and modern direction for cutting images. (Cooper wrote his master's thesis on Eisenstein, and even spent three weeks at the Eisenstein Kabinet in former Leningrad.) *Mission: Impossible*, a cut-to-the-chase action film based on the 1960s American television show, has an emphatically frenetic editing style. The action is engaged by the lighting of a fuse that burns with a white-hot light echoed in the cold bluish-white tones of the film stock. The camera cuts rapidly between cast and crew names rendered in a boldly italic metallic all-cap font that slants forward as if travelling at high velocity, and action grabs from the film itself. The overall editorial effect, appropriately enough, is of lightning speed, excitement and urgency.

In many ways, film titles have everything to do with the parallel genre of music videos. It comes as no surprise that Cooper's most stunning and effective title sequences have been created in collaboration with filmmakers like David Fincher and Mark Pellington, who began their careers directing music videos and understand the tenets of visual compression. According to Cooper, however, no two collaborations are alike. "For me it's less about the project and more about the relationship I have with the client," he says. Sometimes he executes the director's vision, as with the burning-money titles he did for *Dead Presidents* or the straight
32 narrative introduction and end credits to Oliver Stone's *Nixon* (1995). Other times, there is a creative give-and-take that evolves into a shared vision, as in *Seven* ("David and I brainstormed about most of the shots") and *Arlington Road* ("We talked a lot about the threat of domestic terrorism, and just went to some tract housing in Valencia to shoot stereotypical suburban things"). For a designer who has always aspired to directing feature films, spending time with film

OPPOSITE Cooper spent 35 days shooting film for *New Port South* at a high school in Libertyville, Illinois, during the middle of a brutal Midwestern winter. "I've never been in a war," Cooper says, "but having to band together with very little sleep and a crazy production schedule sure felt like it." Photograph by Chuck Hodes/Touchstone Pictures.

20

luminaries like John Frankenheimer and Robert Redford has its benefits. "I can live vicariously through listening to their lives," he notes. "You assume you're going to meet a guru and that they're going to have some special insight, that every word is going to be a gem. But I watch these people struggle."

Separating out who did what on projects is an especially sticky issue when you're working in film. Unlike with more solitary art forms like writing, painting or composing, film is by nature a collaborative effort. Designers are known to cross over and be directors and directors often serve as designers. "I love the challenge of trying to solve something," Cooper admits, "but I don't want to do it by myself. I have always felt insecure about my executional skills, which is maybe why I like to collaborate with other people." Although Cooper acts as the company's centre of creative gravity, he concedes that Imaginary Forces' success is due to the talent of all the designers there, including newer partners like Karin Fong, Mikon van Gastel, Saffron Kenny, Kurt Mattila and Michael Reilly.

In describing Imaginary Forces, Cooper wades into theological waters, quoting biblical themes like "iron sharpening iron" to describe the collaborative process. The company is broken up into creative teams, with each partner leading his or her own core team. Often, people are paired up for the very reason that they disagree in the hope that the creative friction will produce something remarkable and unexpected. "The other biblical principle," remarks Cooper, "is 'Why does the eye say to the hand, I have no use for you?' If someone can make something better, then great."

While it's an admirable – even ambitious – way to think about a company, the reality is that eyes and hands are nowhere without a head. "There's a constant tension as to whether it's Kyle's company or whether he is just part of the greater whole," says Peter Frankfurt, Cooper's friend and one of Imaginary Forces' original cofounders. "More often than not, Kyle is saying 'I know how to make all these pieces fit together. I have this recipe in my head, and none of you know how to work together in the way that I know you should. Just do what I say.'"[10]

Imaginary Forces had a chance to experience a Cooper-less company in 2000 when he took a year's leave to shoot his first feature, a noirish teen drama produced by John Hughes called *New Port South* that takes place – naturally – in American suburbia. Cooper is circumspect in his discussion of the film, which was written by Hughes' 21-year-old son,

James, and takes as its creative inspiration elements of *The Dead Zone* and Stanley Kubrick's oeuvre. The film, which had a short release in theatres around Chicago in 2001 before going to DVD in early 2002, possesses some vintage Cooper elements: menace, moral ambiguity and a plot that features graphic design and photography in starring roles. Shot in the chilly, flat landscape to the north of Chicago, *New Port South* has an atmospheric bleakness that is almost able to mask its muddled, cryptic storyline about teenagers rebelling against an overly legalistic high-school regime. Although Cooper maintains that he is still on good terms with Hughes father and son, he makes it clear that he was not given enough control in the final edit of the half-a-million feet of film he shot for the project. "There are all kinds of things that haunt me," he says, "either because I took on too many things or because the producer was expecting something different. I want to go back and fix them."

Although the chances that a controlling visionary like Cooper would be entirely satisfied with the constraints put on a film by an unrelentingly upbeat producer like John Hughes, or a company like Disney, are pretty slim, he says the experience – which he describes as having been as intense as going to war – was invaluable, and that he is a much better director for it.

After his year in the field, Cooper returned to Imaginary Forces, but just long enough to realize that his growing directorial and design aspirations were being countered by the demands of running a large company. In spring 2003, as this book was going to press, Cooper sold his share in the business and began a period of experimentation, exploring possibilities as an independent director and as a collaborator with Garson Yu, a long-time friend from his Yale days and founder of the Los Angeles-based motion-graphics firm yu+co. "When you play with other people, it's always more fun," he says.

Asked whether he would prefer to direct films rather than create title sequences or commercials, Cooper is thoughtful: "Before I go into another feature, I want to be more cautious about a lot of things. I'm not even sure that a live-action director career is more important to me. Design is design. There isn't any kind of work that I think should be treated as lesser."

Selected Work

True Lies

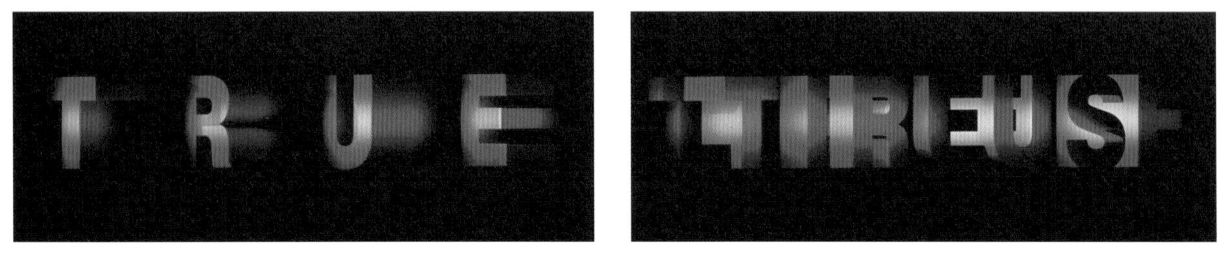

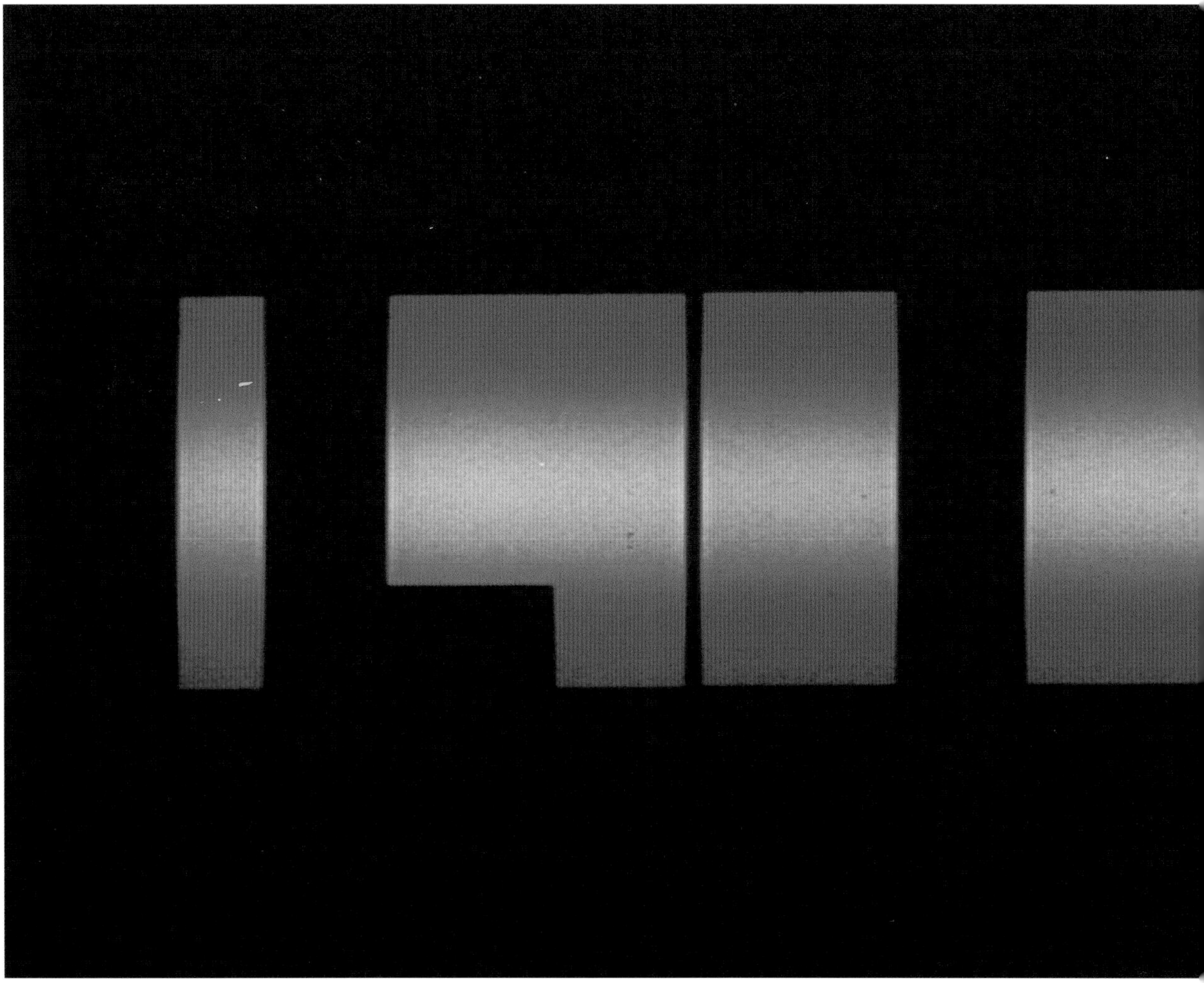

Director – James Cameron, 1994
Titles – Kyle Cooper (dir.) for RGA/LA

Created in Los Angeles three years after Cooper relocated from New York, the main titles for James Cameron's *True Lies* are typical of the R/Greenberg approach to motion graphics first made famous in *Altered States* and *Alien*: word-based conceptual formations.

"The Greenberg school was more about slow reveals and simple ideas," admits Cooper, who in this instance directed a simple but effective sequence to this action movie about a character's duplicitous life as a CIA agent (even his wife doesn't know his true profession until halfway through the movie). Using large bluish metallic type on a black background, the word "True" slowly rotates in three-dimensional space to reveal the word "Lies" created by the dark background between the letterforms. An antecedent to later works that rely on what can best be called "typographic method acting", Cooper's *True Lies* sequence succeeds in addressing the movie's oxymoronic title and the character's ethical slipperiness with a minimum of means.

Dead Presidents

Directors – The Hughes Brothers, 1995
Titles – Kyle Cooper (dir.) for RGA/LA

Hollywood directors have been known to burn through money during film productions, but few have had the pleasure of doing so literally. In this title for a film about an armoured-car heist, Cooper and his R/Greenberg colleagues were given the idea of using burning money by the directors, the Hughes Brothers. Burning money cinematographically proved to be more difficult than expected, however. "We had to experiment with different paper stocks and ways to reprint money at a larger scale," explains Cooper. "We shot burning money for two days." The sequence begins with quick flashes of the robbers, black men with reverse-minstrelsy white faces.

Then the burning begins with a close-up of George Washington – that iconic dead (white) president – whose familiar face becomes consumed in flames. Also up in smoke, in typical Cooper fashion, are other treasured national symbols such as God and country.

A HUGHES BROTHERS FILM

DAVID BARRY GRAY

MICHAEL IMPERIOLI

JENIFER LEWIS

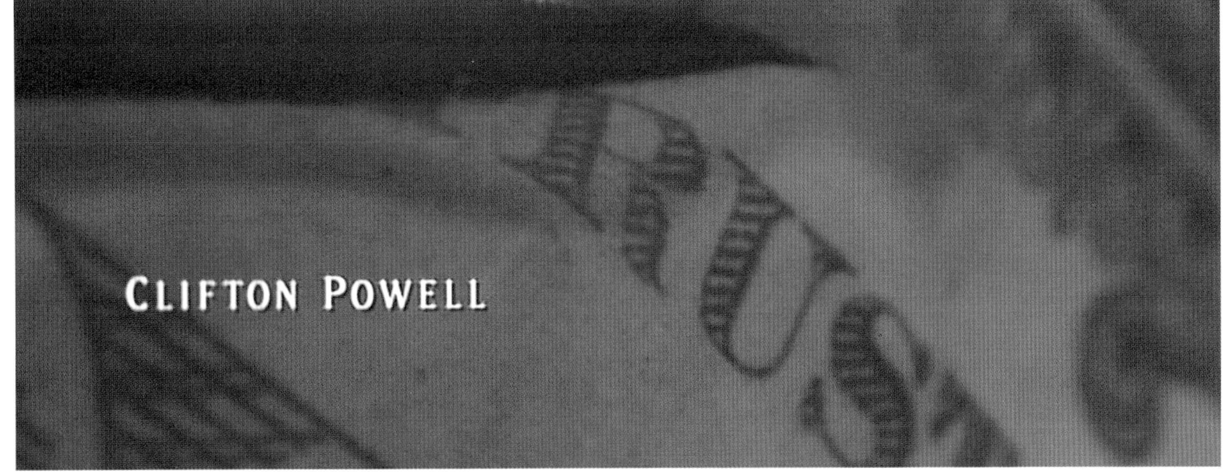
CLIFTON POWELL

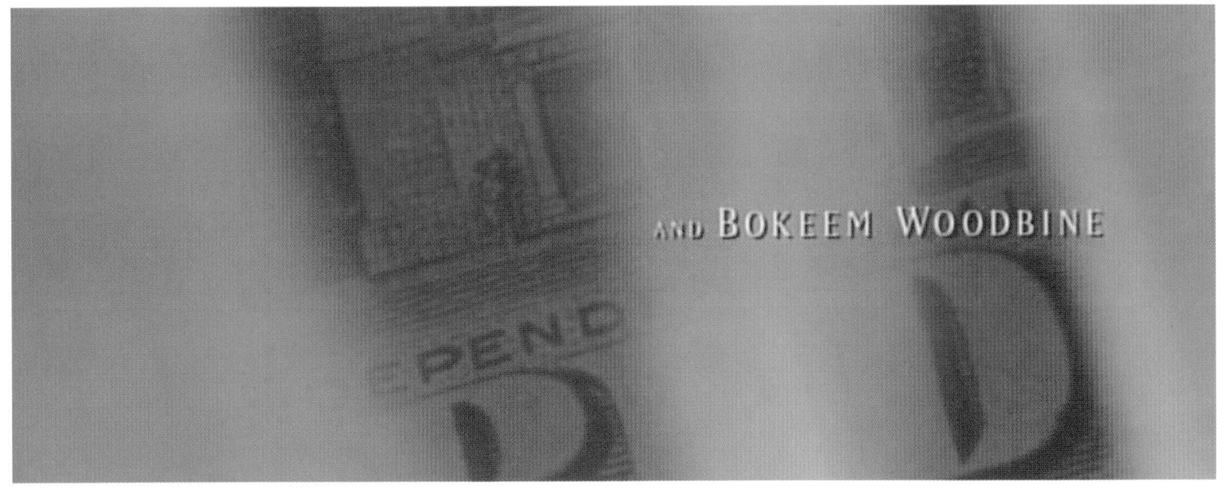
AND BOKEEM WOODBINE

B
210057

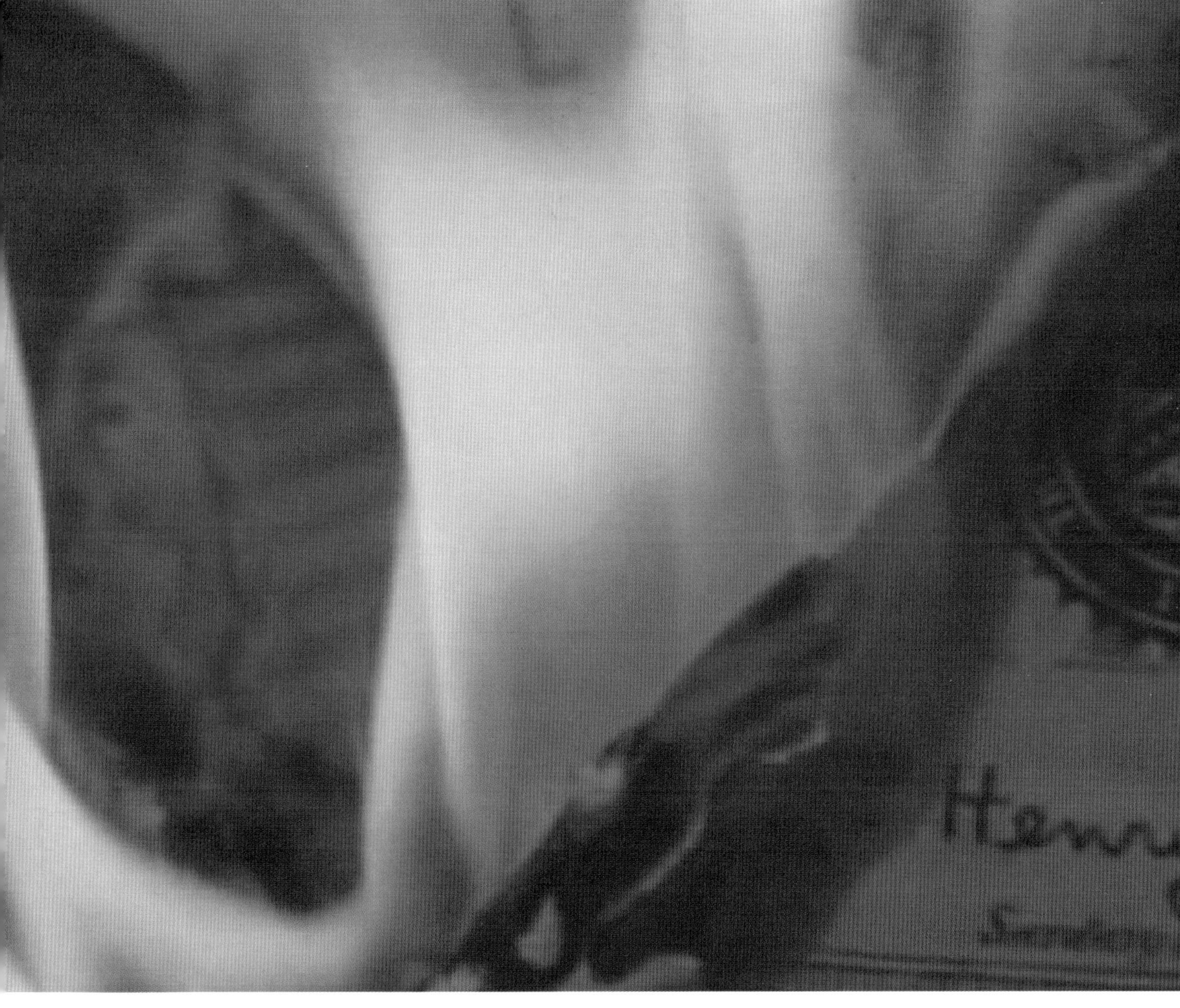

Nixon

Director – Oliver Stone, 1995
Titles – Kyle Cooper (dir.)
for Imaginary Forces

Sometimes a distinctly cinematic approach to titles is necessary, as in the case of Oliver Stone's *Nixon*, which has a cast and crew so large that the credits appear directly over the opening scenes of the movie itself. "Stone was staggeringly specific about what he wanted us to do," admits Cooper, whose touch as creative director is seen most readily in the addition of a quote from the New Testament about the price of worldly success – a poignant juxtaposition with the following scenes, which show the legendary break-in at Watergate and its disastrous consequences on the Nixon presidency. Cooper also cleverly casts the illuminated round lens of a film projector as the "o" in "Nixon"; this also reads as an allusion to the flashlights carried by the Watergate intruders and the bright figurative spotlight cast on Nixon and his cabinet members during the following investigation. The plain white all-cap titles seem to carry the weight of unadorned history, although Stone interestingly includes a disclaimer up front that the film is an "interpretation" of events.

"For what is a man profited, if he shall gain the whole world, and lose his own soul?"

– Matthew 16:26

N I X N

N I O N

STARRING (IN

PHABETICAL ORDER)

Seven

Director – David Fincher, 1995
Titles – Kyle Cooper (dir.) for RGA/LA
Storyboard art – Wayne Coe

Cooper's rising star was a dark one if you consider his opening titles for David Fincher's suspense film *Seven*, which combined "scratchy" type with disturbing Joel Peter Witkinesque photography and the heavy industrial music of Nine Inch Nails into a distinct cultural moment. After brainstorming with director Fincher and deciding that the visual direction would be closed and obsessive, like the inwardly revolving thoughts of a madman, Cooper worked with storyboard artist Wayne Coe on visualizations that would be shot in live action. Also a filmmaking and horror-genre enthusiast, Coe storyboarded frame-by-frame scenarios of the serial killer John Doe scribbling in his journal, blotting out faces in photographs, sewing pages together and, most disturbingly, shaving his fingerprints off. The resulting filmed title sequence is insistently handcrafted to the exclusion of any digital intervention except the nonlinear editing. (The closing credits, in fact, are constructed of hair, dirt, dead insects and nail clippings taped directly to an optical.)

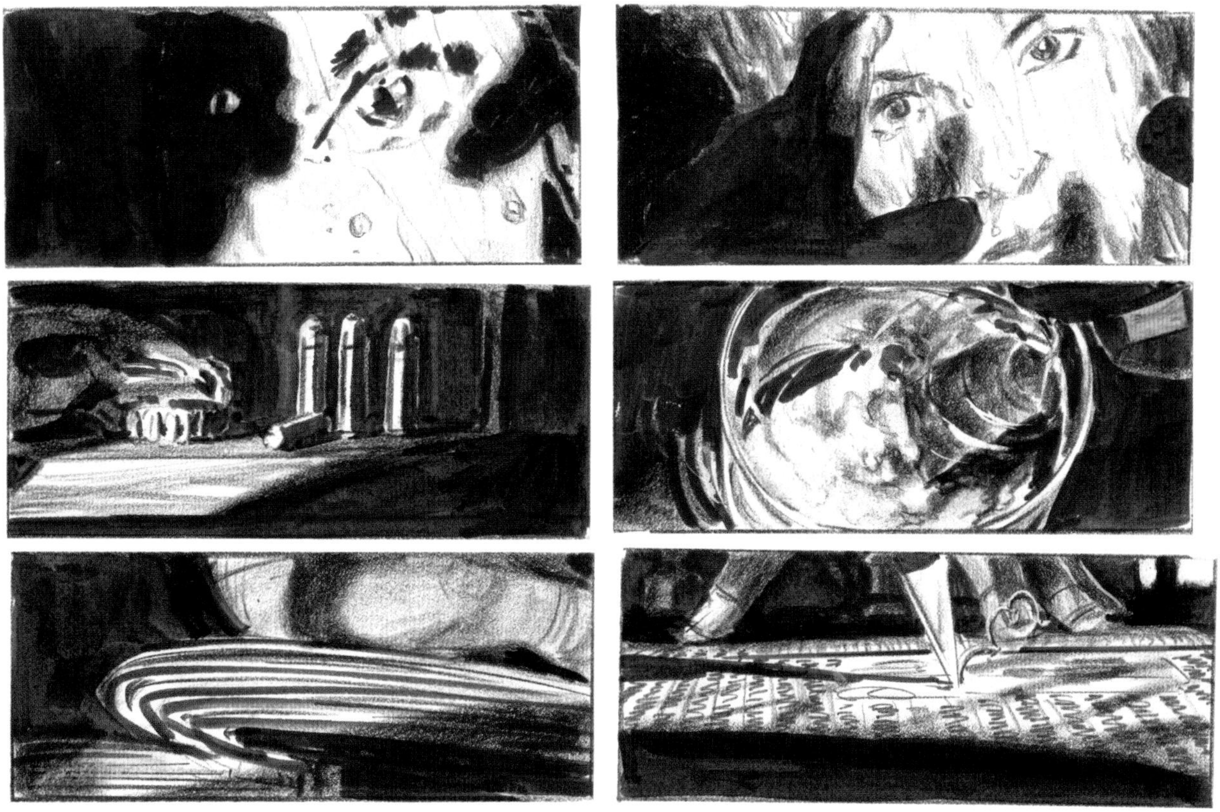

During the creative process, Cooper admits to having found some commonality with the film's killer, John Doe, while scrabbling around in his basement at all hours for disgusting titbits to add to the end credits. "It's okay to be obsessive about work," he says. "Unless of course you're killing people as a result."

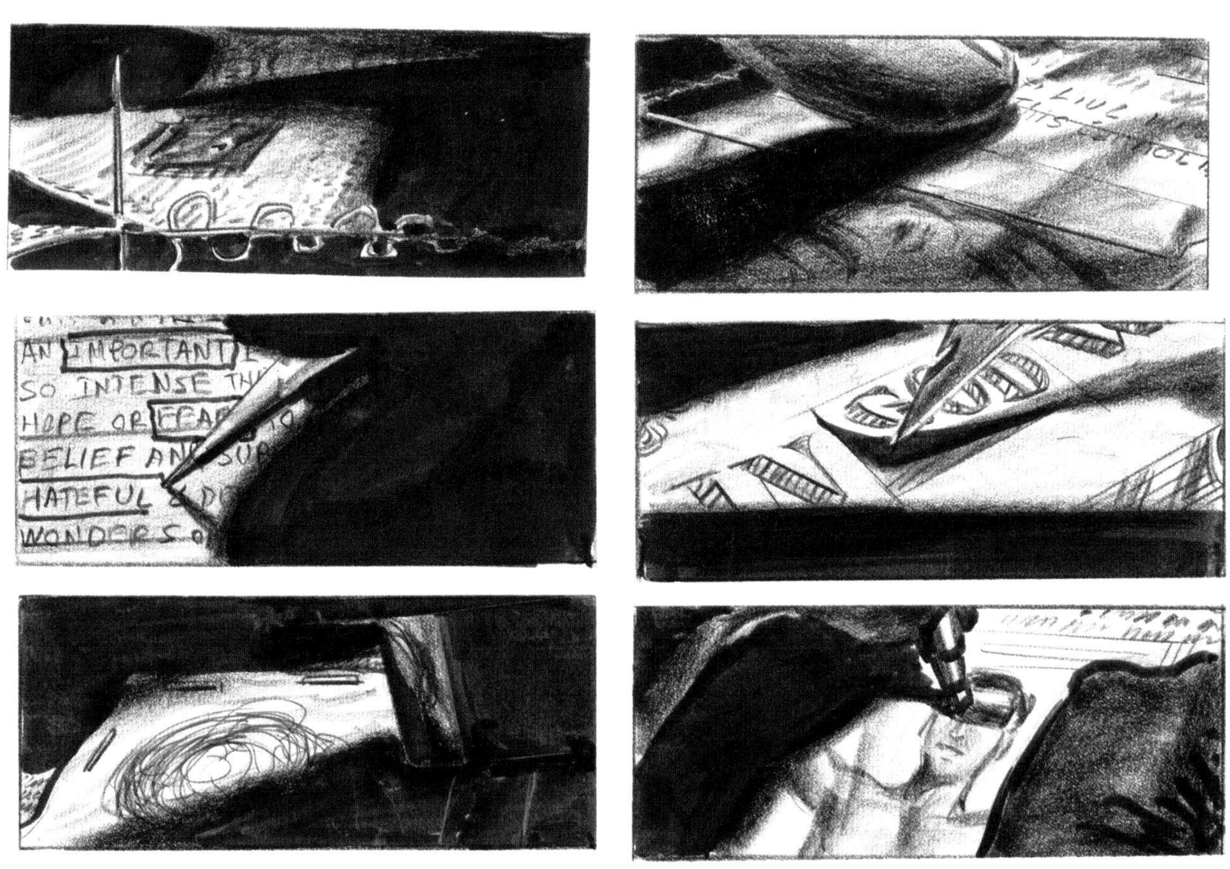

38

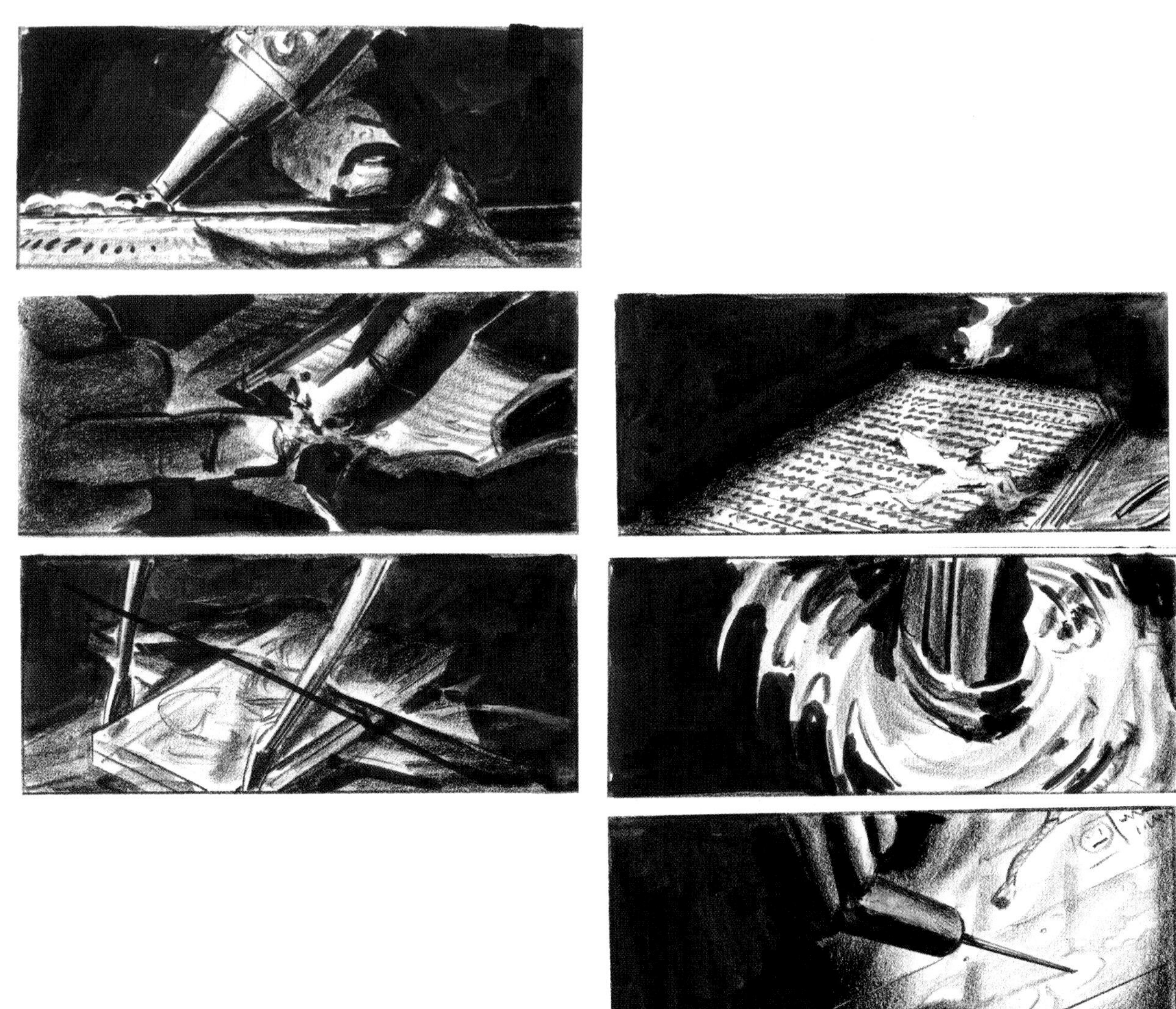

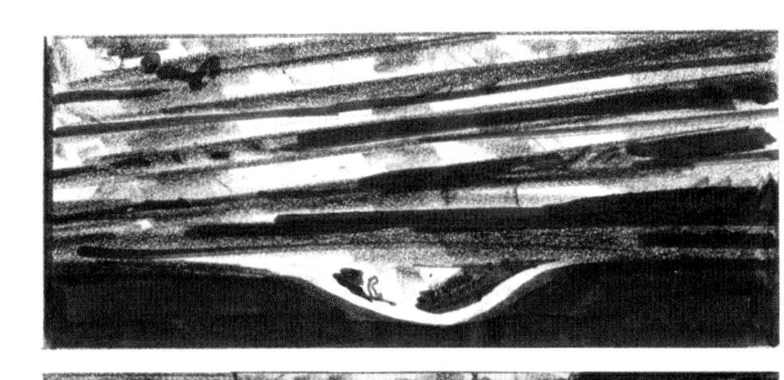

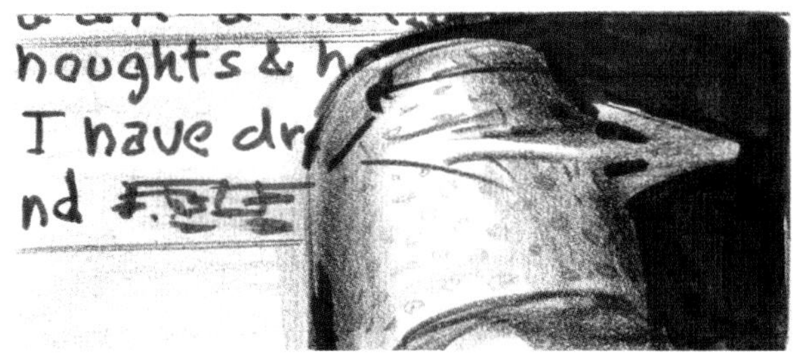
houghts & h
I have dr
nd

40

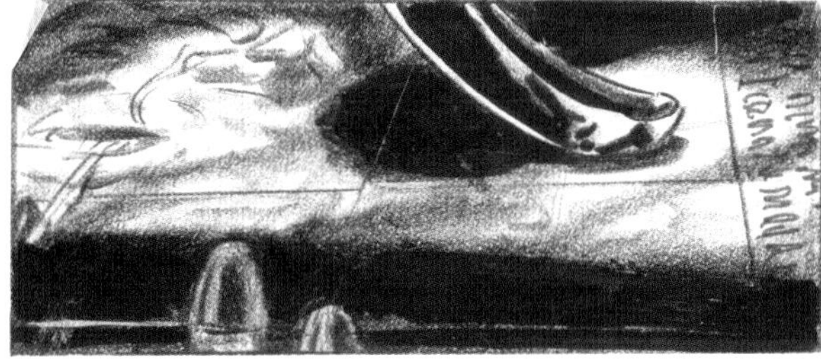

Gotti

Director – Robert Harmon, 1996 [TV]
Titles – Kyle Cooper (creative dir.)
for Imaginary Forces

For this HBO film about the legendary Mafia crime boss John Gotti, Cooper creative-directed a visual approach that is reminiscent of police blotters and New York's criminal underworld. The camera pans over a police blotter that features the mug shots of Mafia goodfellas, which appear in negative until a blinding flash of light reverses them out into normal photos; once the camera moves on to a different visage, the mug shot returns to its negative and the visual sequence continues. Halfway through the titles, the camera fixes on the face of actor Armando Assante, who plays the lead character. Although the camera moves on to seek out other mug shots, Gotti's photo does not return to its original negative, but rather stays distinctly reversed out – an indication that the film's narrative revolves around this character.

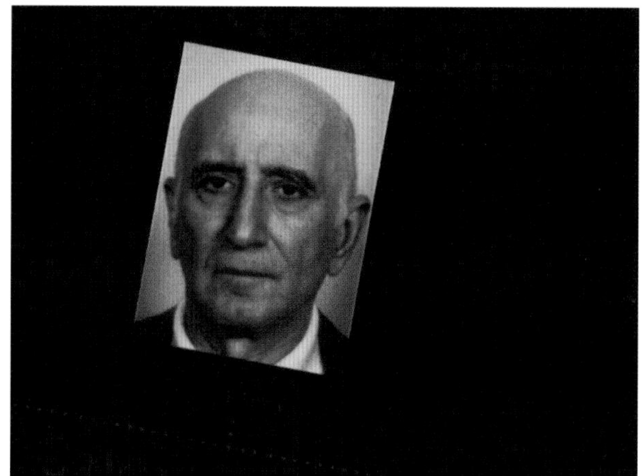

ALBERTA WATSON
AL WAXMAN

The Island of Dr. Moreau

Director – John Frankenheimer, 1996
Titles – Kyle Cooper (dir.) for RGA/LA
Storyboard art – Wayne Coe

From the very beginning of visualizing the title sequence for *The Island of Dr. Moreau*, Cooper knew that the theme of biological mutation would be paramount. Through a series of explorations with storyboard artist Wayne Coe, Cooper honed his sequence from an initial direction of eyes splitting and multiplying as if going through cell mitosis (pp. 46–7) to the final direction, which begins by pulling the viewer through a series of animal irises. In this way, Cooper intimates the film's plot – inter-species biological tinkering gone awry. The resulting sequence is aggressively paced to a driving hip-hop beat, a hallucinatory combination of medical and cellular imagery from a number of stock sources that could possibly pose serious problems to epileptics in the audience.

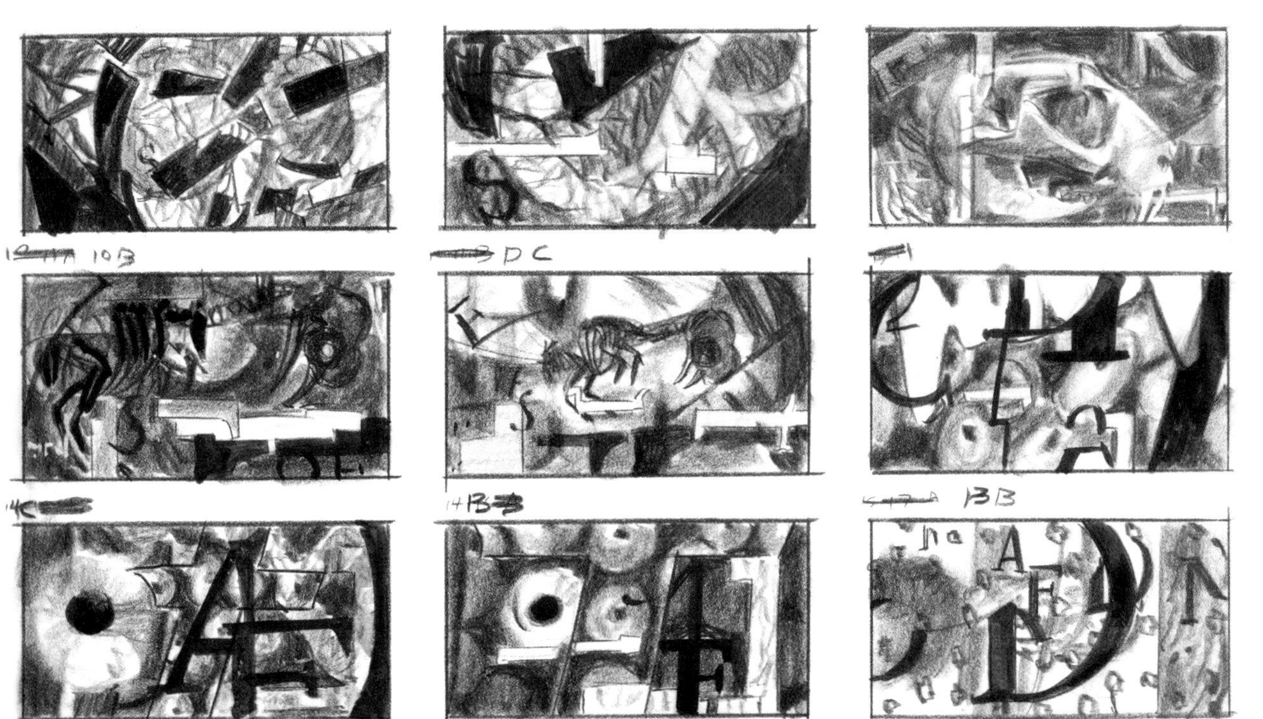

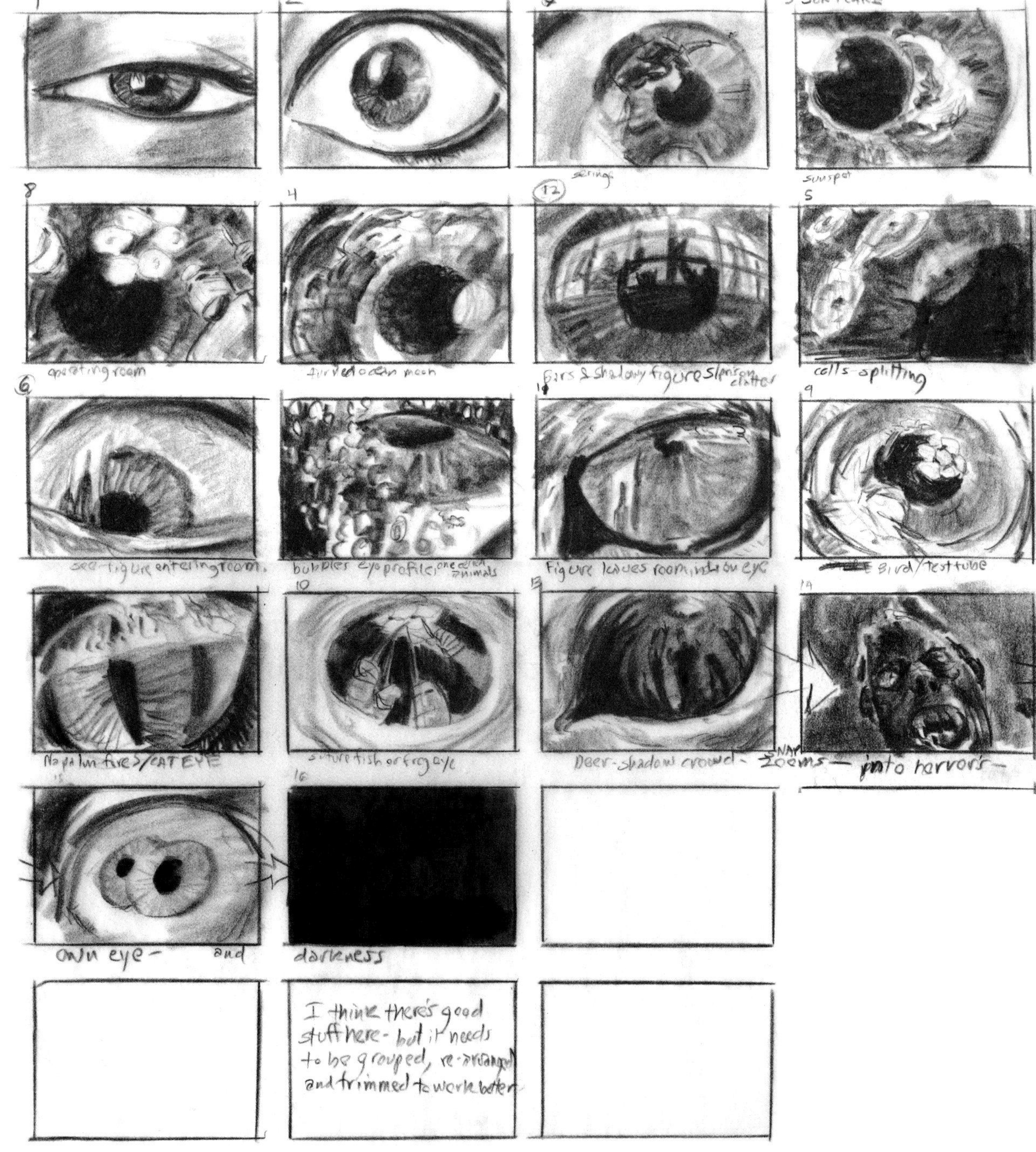
SUN FLARE
syringe
sunspot
operating room
Airless ocean moon
Bars & shadowy figures
cells splitting
see figure entering room
bubbles eye profile
Figure leaves room
bird/test tube
Napalm fires/CAT EYE
fish or frog eye
Deer-shadow crowd
Zooms — into horrors —
own eye — and
darkness
I think there's good
stuff here - but it needs
to be grouped, re-arranged
and trimmed to work better

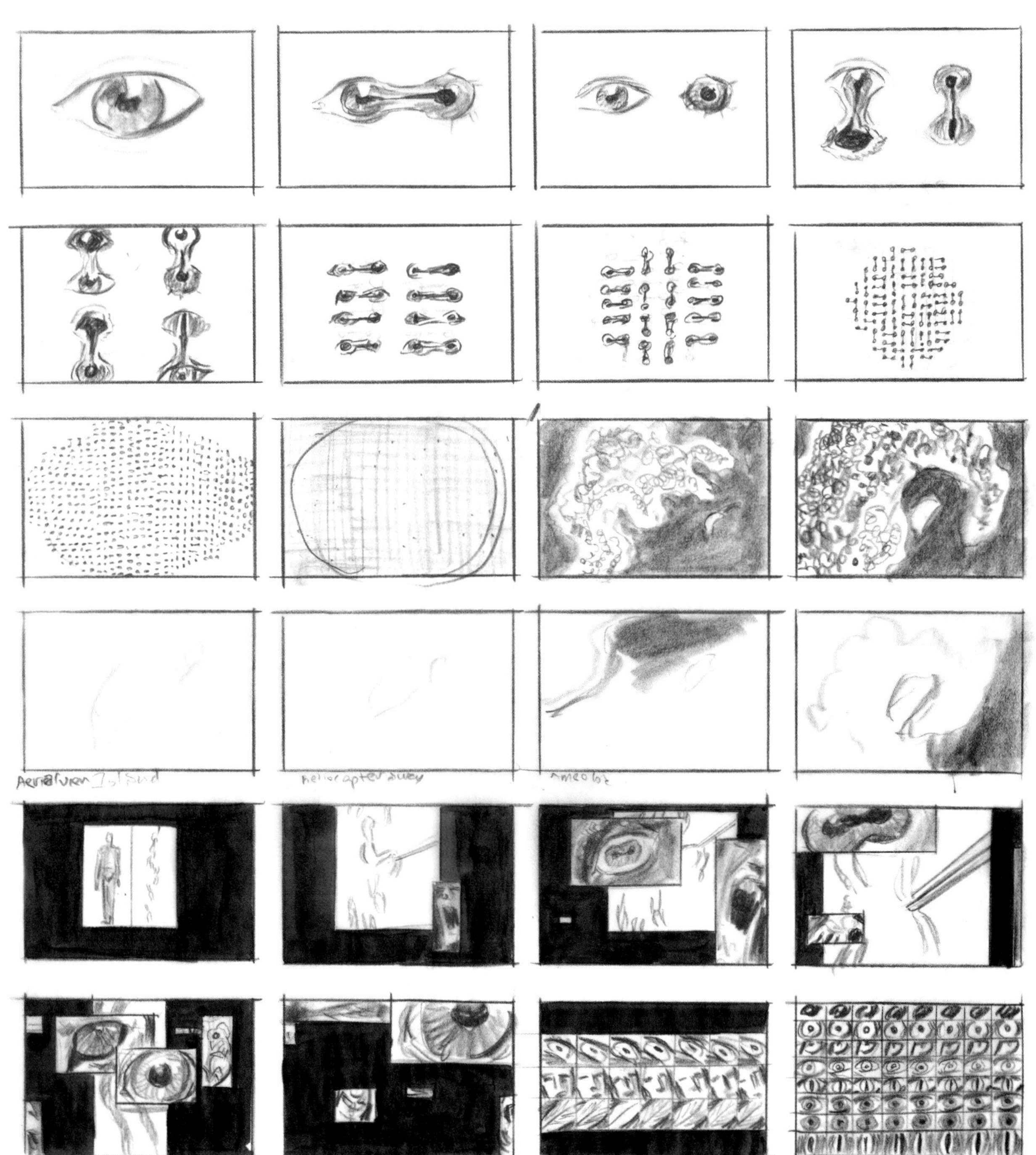

"I usually do things with scissors and scan them in," says Cooper, who admits to a preference for hands-on, low-tech approaches to projects. In *The Island of Dr. Moreau*, Cooper uncharacteristically turned to Illustrator for help to pull out the edge points of the credit typefaces to render them figuratively red in tooth and claw. The credits appear at first normal, but then the serifs spike out dangerously and begin to mutate and splinter as if they, too, were going through an out-of-control metamorphosis.

MOREAU

MOREAU

THE ISLAND OF DR. MOREAU

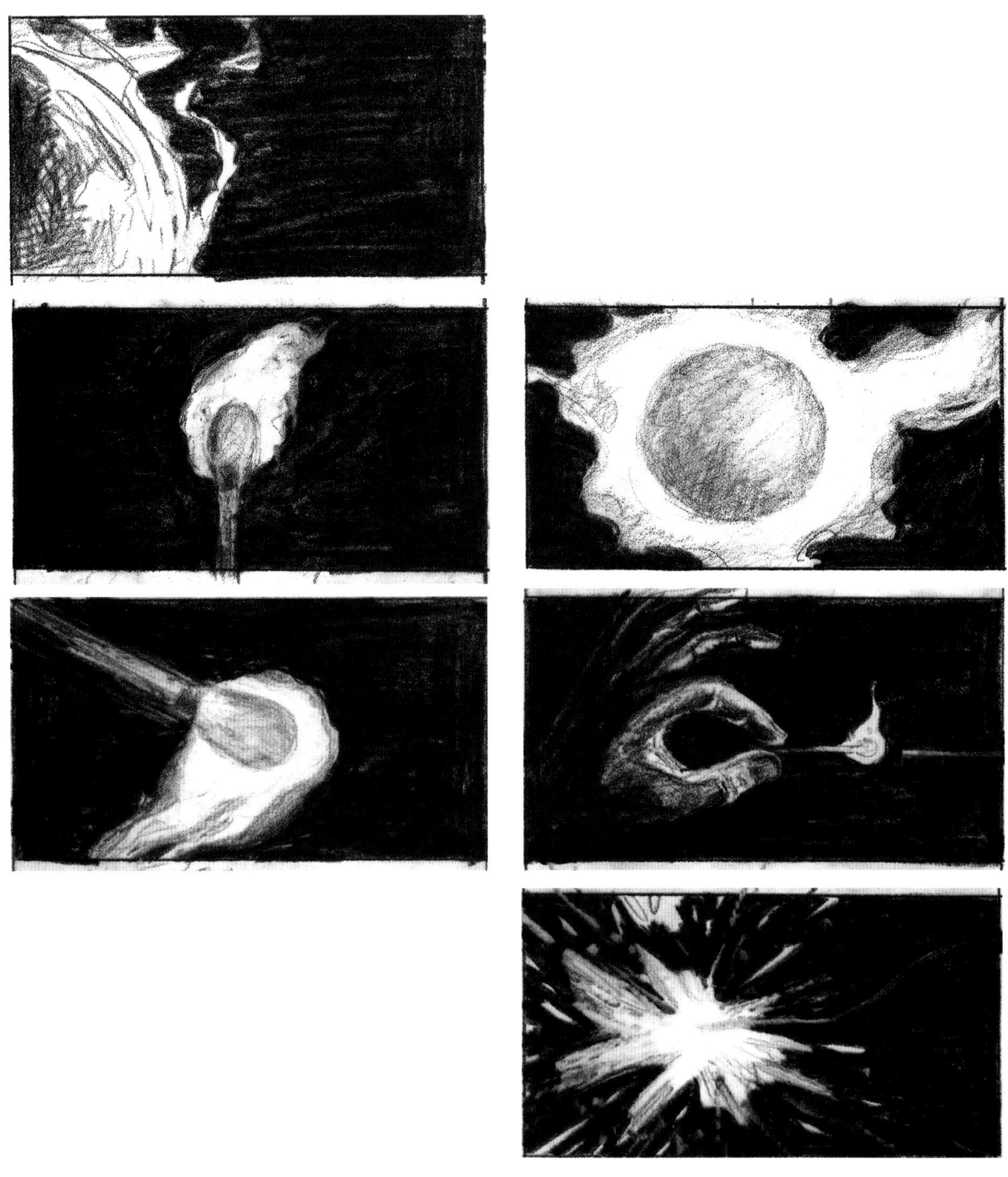

Director – Brian De Palma, 1996
Titles – Kyle Cooper (dir.)
for Imaginary Forces

The opening sequence to *Mission: Impossible* takes its cue from the 1960s television show, which always begins with a fuse being lit as a trigger for action sequences. An emphasis is put on the flame and sparks by placing them tightly in frame and against a black background. As scenes from the film flash on and off the screen, interspersed with metal-reminiscent credits that glint with speed and urgency, the fuse sparks on to the end of its logical course – a visual explosion that introduces the title of the movie in bold italic serif type.

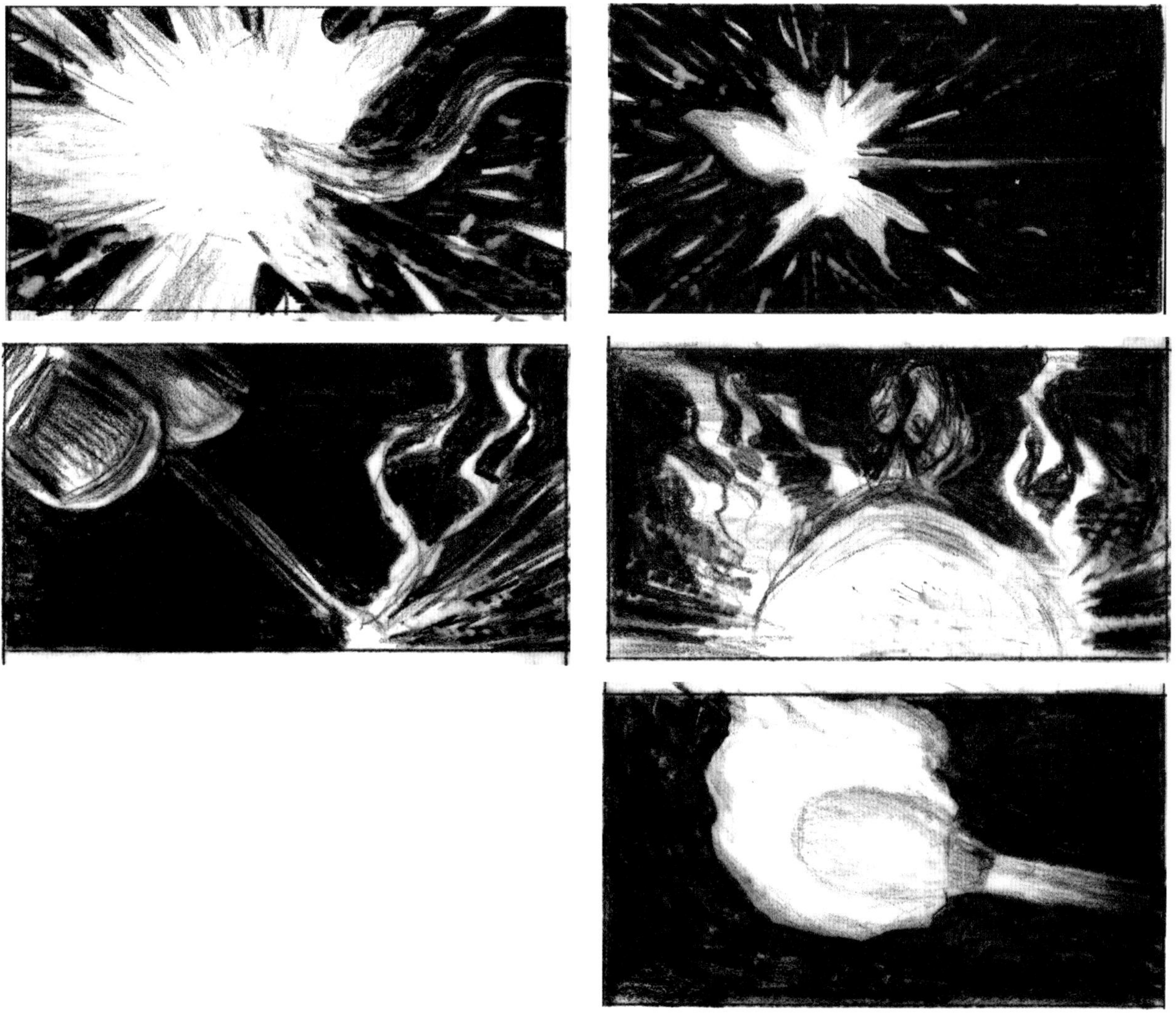

A CRUISE/WAGNER
PRODUCTION

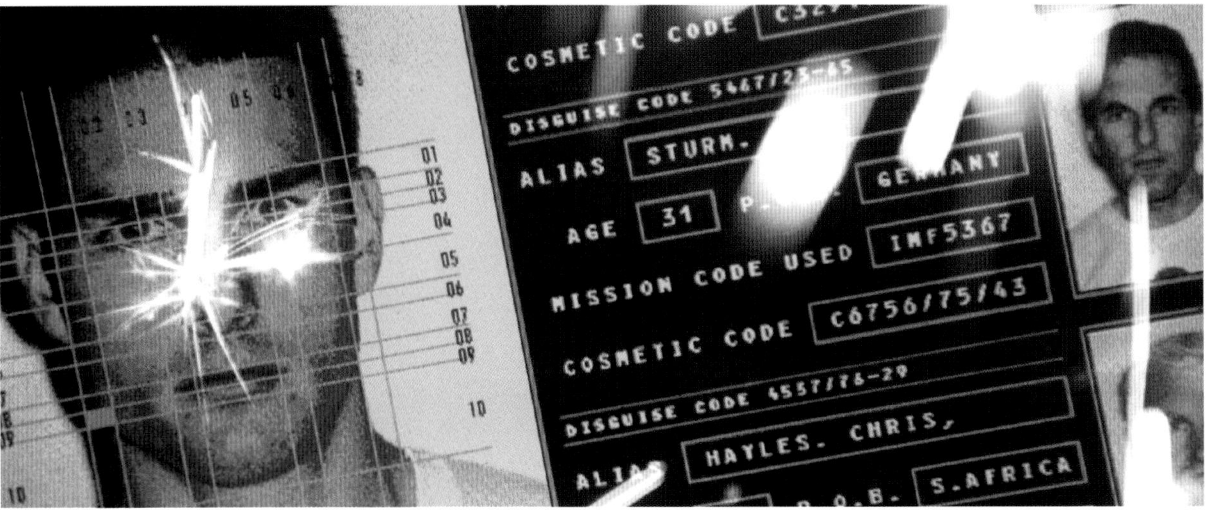
COSMETIC CODE
ALIAS STURM.
AGE 31
MISSION CODE USED IMF5367
COSMETIC CODE C6756/75/43
DISGUISE CODE 4557/76-29
HAYLES. CHRIS,
S.AFRICA

MISSION
IMPOSSIBLE

IMPOSSIBLE

Twister

Director – Jan De Bont, 1996
Titles – Kyles Cooper (creative dir.)
for RGA/LA

Cooper's adolescent pastime of taking words from the dictionary and rendering them in a graphic form to illustrate their meaning was good training for creating main titles such as this one for *Twister*, a film about tornado chasers and their attempts to film a massive storm.

The sequence's creative direction takes much from Cooper's early graphic experimentation, and revolves around a digitally manipulated typeface that appears one minute in the vortex of a storm cloud and is gone with the wind in the next, breaking away like so much trailer-park debris. The massive bluish-grey cloud, hovering mid-screen as if in the eye of the storm, is accompanied by an ominous wall of sound that whips into a windy frenzy to blow the main titles to smithereens.

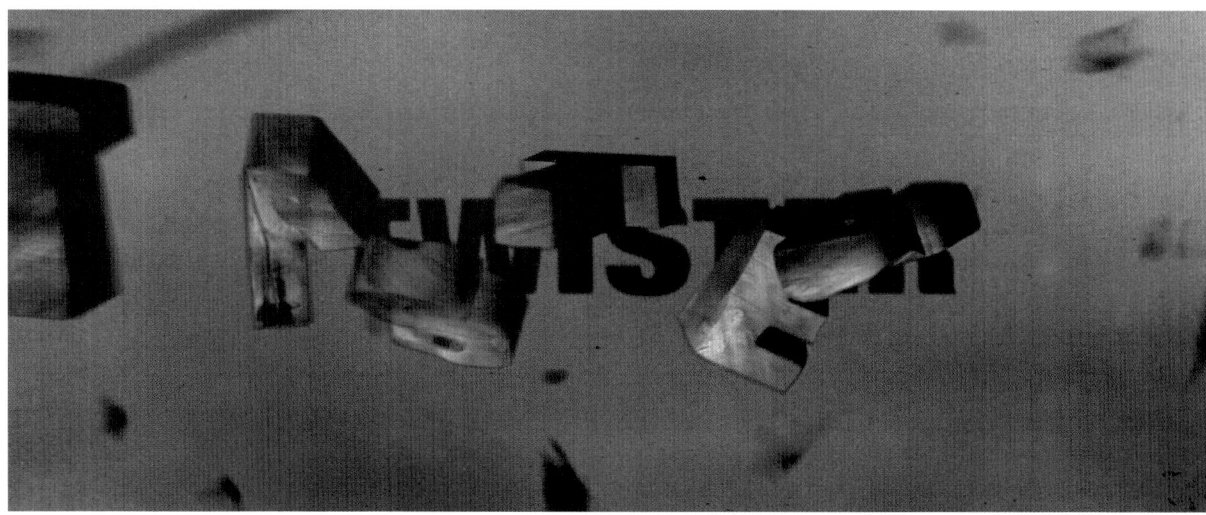

TW

TWISTER

Donnie Brasco

Director – Mike Newell, 1997
Titles – Kyle Cooper (dir.)
for Imaginary Forces

One of the first main titles to be done under the Imaginary Forces name, *Donnie Brasco* is a micro-narrative so moody and evocative that it had one *New Yorker* critic praising it above the film itself. Using a combination of predominantly black-and-white and colour stills shot in surveillance style – complete with Kodak markings and grease-pencil scribblings – Cooper choreographs an unsettling sequence about friendship, betrayal and the implosion of relationships caught in the middle. Accompanied by a delicate piece of music by Beethoven, the gritty still images become animated thanks to a carefully choreographed edit that favours slow fades punctuated by rapid-cut action sequences and the occasional piece of live footage. The titles begin and end with a view of Johnny Depp's dark-ringed eyes looking from outside – an imposter cop in the midst of New York wise guys.

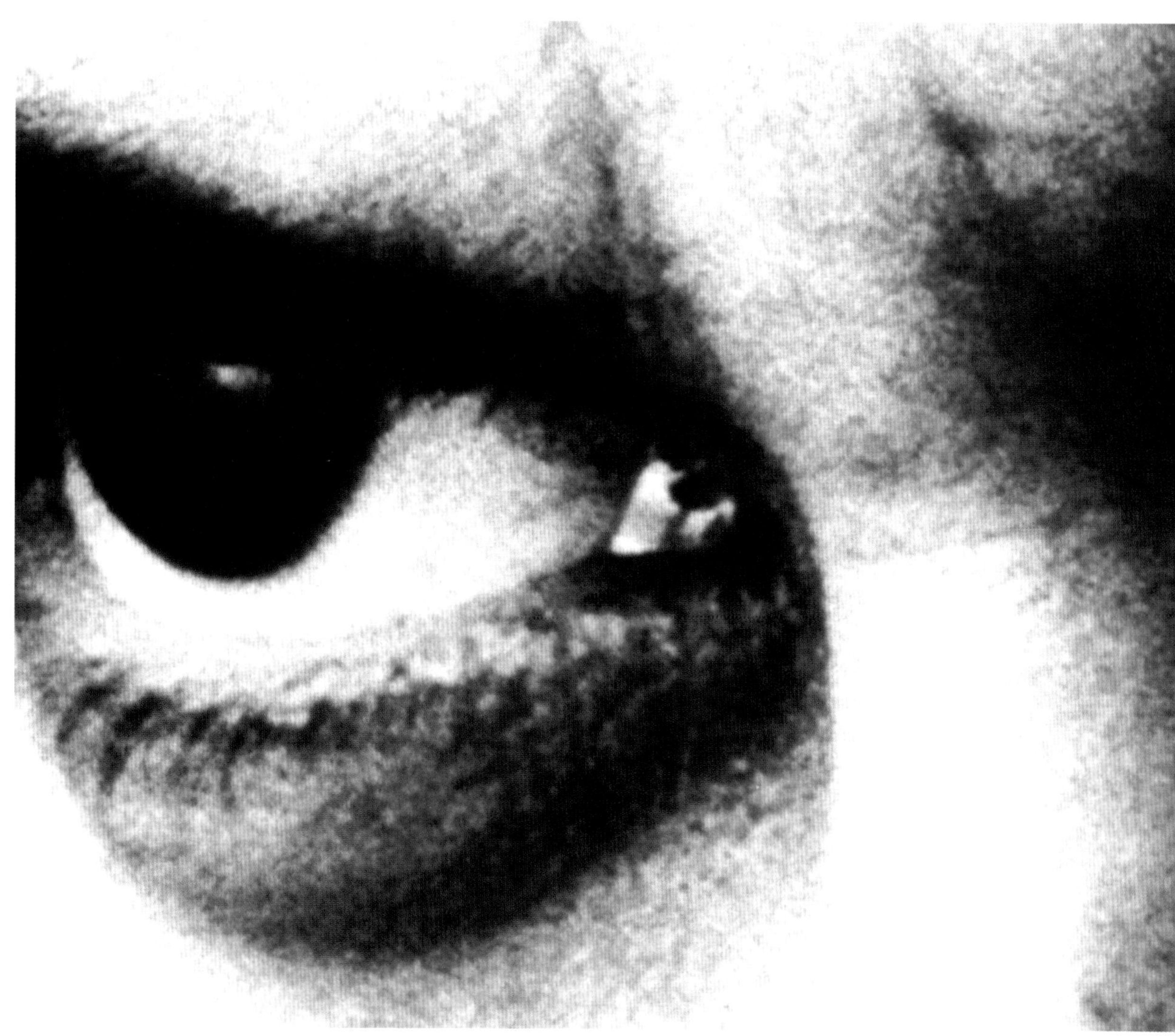

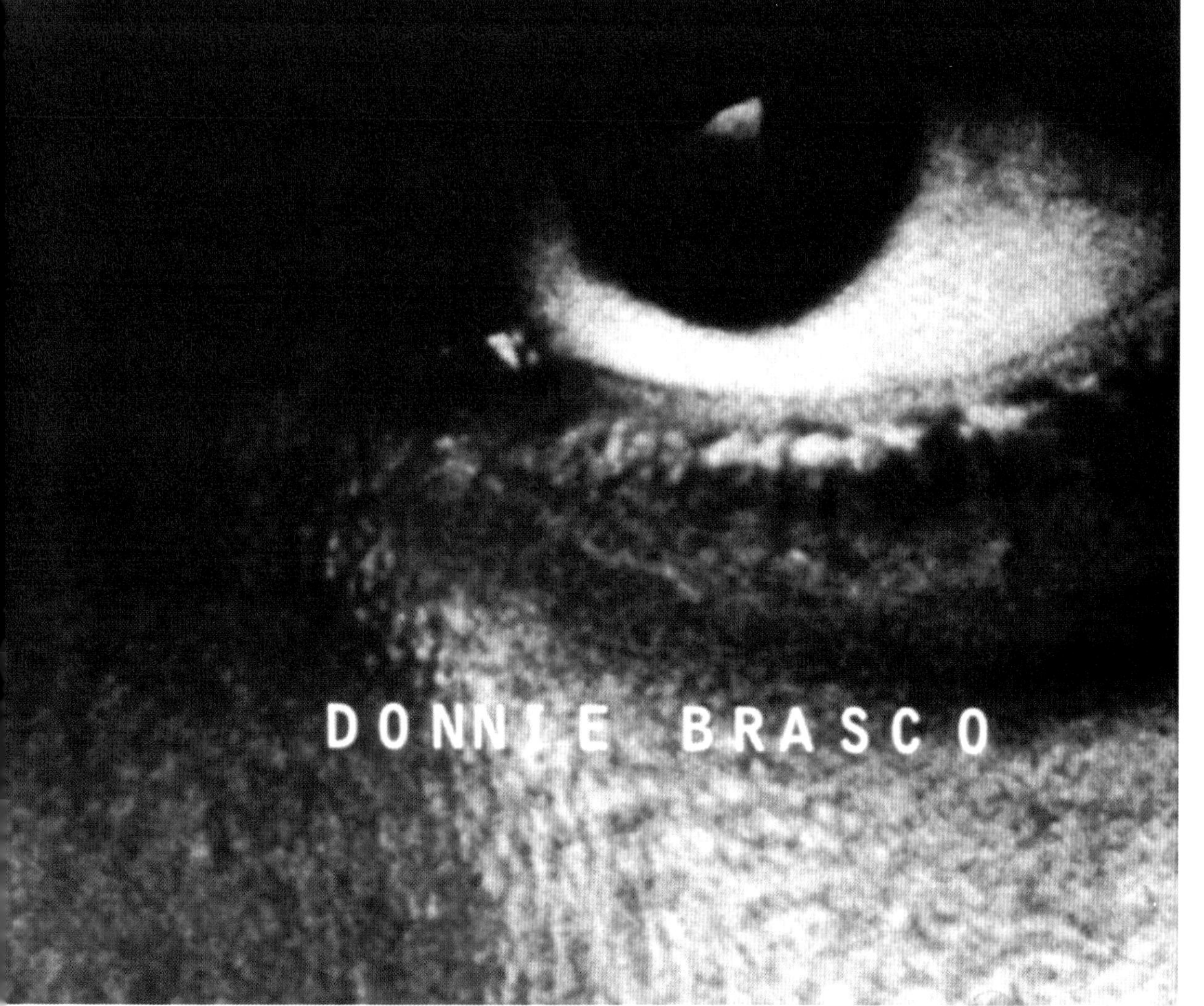
DONNIE BRASCO

JAMES RUSSO

EXECUTIVE
BUDD CARR AND ALLAN MASON

2 KODAK 5063
PRODUCTION DESIGNED BY
DONALD GRAHAM BURT

DIRECTOR OF PHOTOGRAPHY
PETER SOVA

PRODUCED BY

LOUIS DiGIA

GAIL MUTRUX

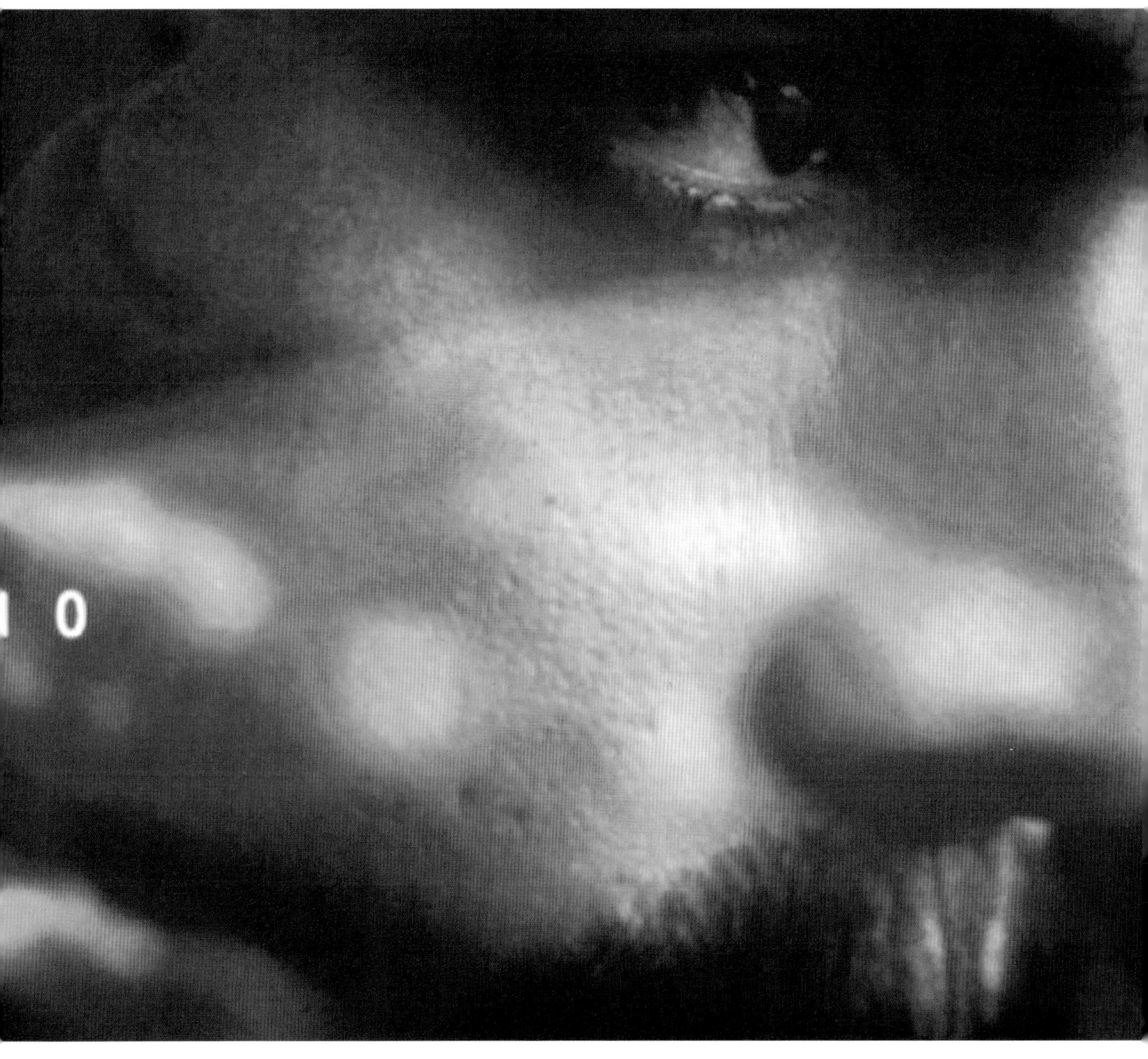

Flubber

Director – Les Mayfield, 1997
Titles – Kyle Cooper (dir.)
for Imaginary Forces

Cooper's sensitivity to typography – and his practice of hiring designers who share his obsession with type – has become a hallmark of many Imaginary Forces credit sequences. This main title for Disney's *Flubber* is another prime example of Cooper's "type casting". In the instance of *Flubber*, which concerns an inventor who creates a rubbery substance that helps people to fly, the names of the film's cast and crew swirl around the screen in a playful way, forming credits that look like mathematical and chemical equations. Chains of chemical bonds, twisting helixes and graphic notations bounce around like the brainstorms of some irrepressible inventor, their manic motion perhaps unwittingly replicating that of the film's notoriously hyper star, Robin Williams.

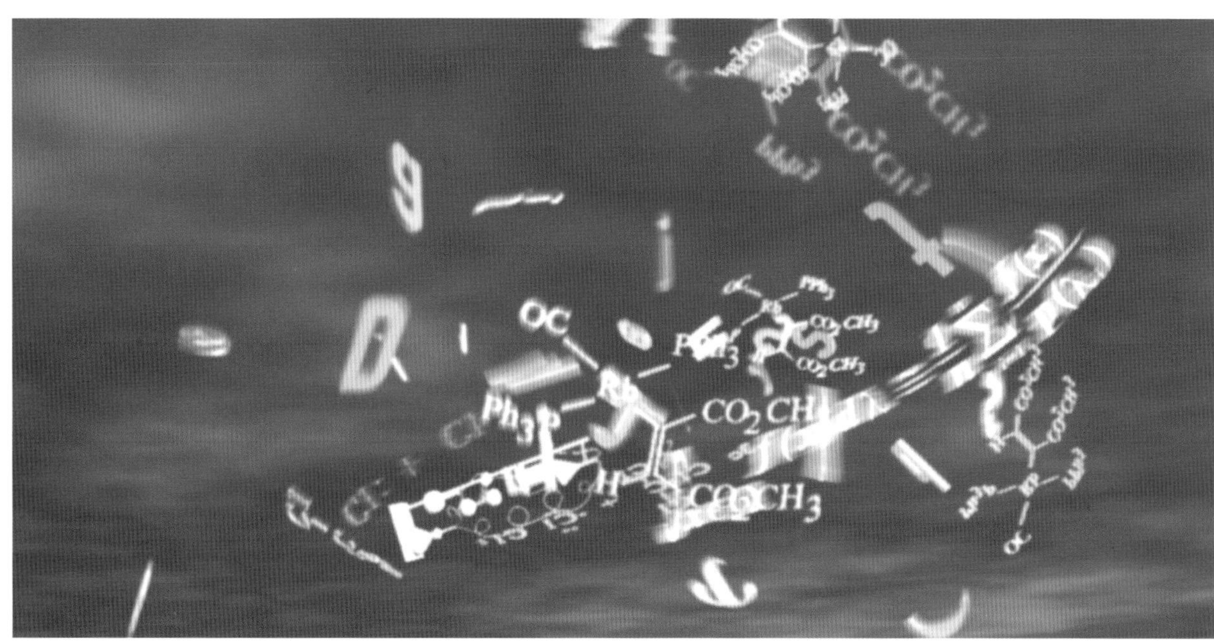

(r)obin Williams

FLU

BER

George Wallace

Director – John Frankenheimer, 1997 [TV]
Titles – Kyle Cooper (creative dir.)
for RGA/LA

Cooper created several main titles for the late director John Frankenheimer, including this Emmy-nominated sequence for a cable television film on the racist southern politician George Wallace. The red-white-and-blue American flag serves as a screen upon which scenes from America's racist past flash. Stark black-and-white photographs and film clips of segregation and racial violence contrast with close-ups of the Declaration of Independence, particularly the phrase "life, liberty and the pursuit of happiness". The names of main cast and crew appear in a blocky and notably white serifed type that seems solid until the credits scatter in all directions, a graphic allusion to the issues of Civil Rights that splintered northern and southern culture in the early 1960s.
In one sequence, the name of the actor Gary Sinise, who plays George Wallace, disassembles into its constituent letters – the letter cluster "sin" tellingly rising from "Sinise".

a JOHN
FRANKENHEIMER
film

GEORGE
WALLACE

WILLIAM SANDERSON
Life, Liberty

Mimic

Director – Guillermo Del Toro, 1997
Titles – Kyle Cooper (dir.)
for Imaginary Forces

Similar in detail and obsessiveness to *Seven* is Cooper's direction for the main titles to *Mimic*. Rather than scraping around on his own floors for dead bugs, however, Cooper travelled to insect-collecting shows to find the perfect specimens to embody the eerie atmosphere of an entomologist's laboratory gone horribly wrong. Insects dappled with intricate patterns are pinned on specimen cards; glassine envelopes hold the remains of torn butterfly wings; beetles come to life and lower-case credits replicate endlessly across the screen, giving a visceral sense of the film's story about a plague that has created human-sized moths. Cooper's favourite leitmotif, the eye, is played up in Man Ray-reminiscent tableaux comprising black-and-white eyes cut from photographs that are pinned and surrealistically wriggle under the harsh light of the researcher's lamp.

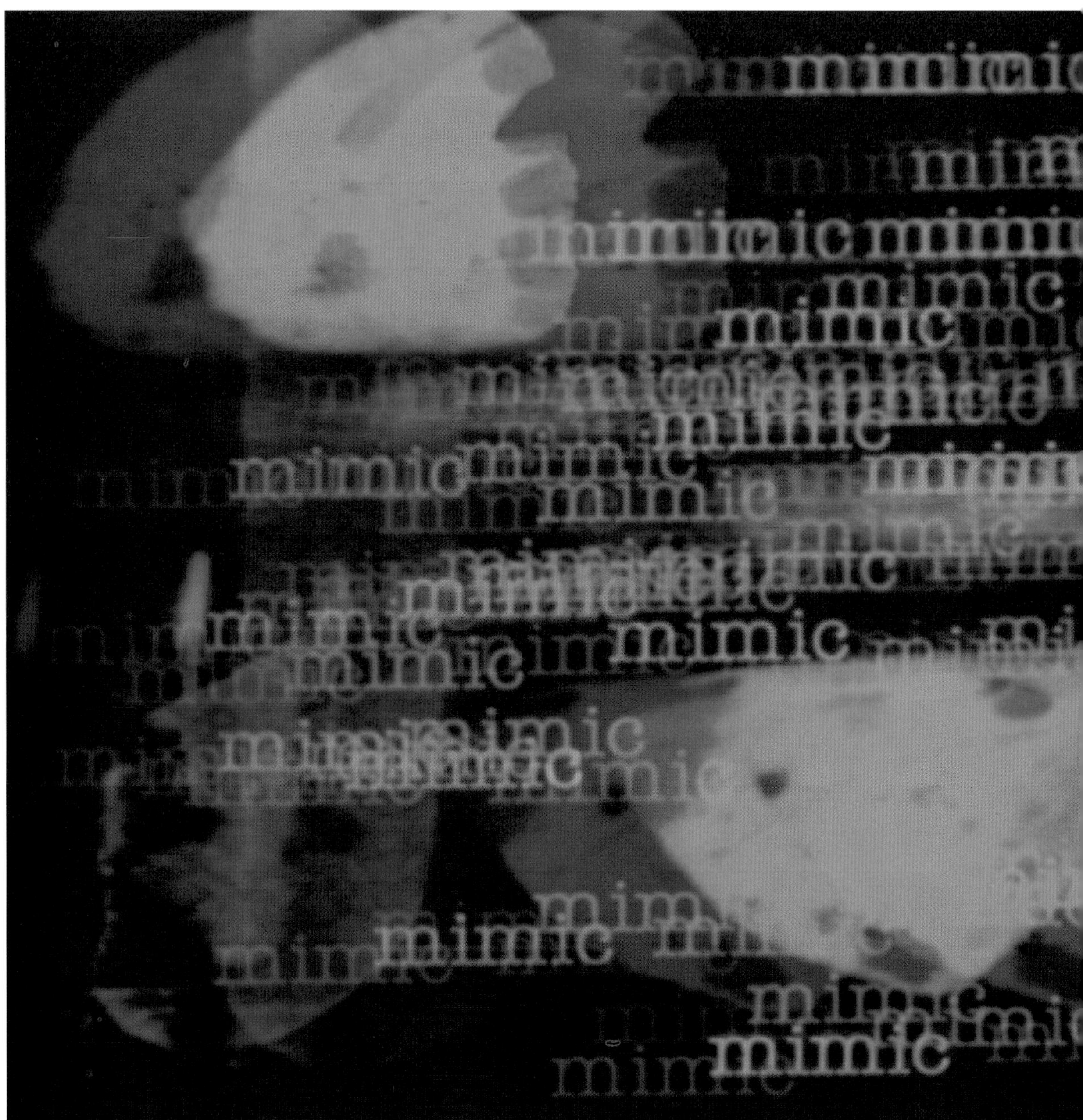

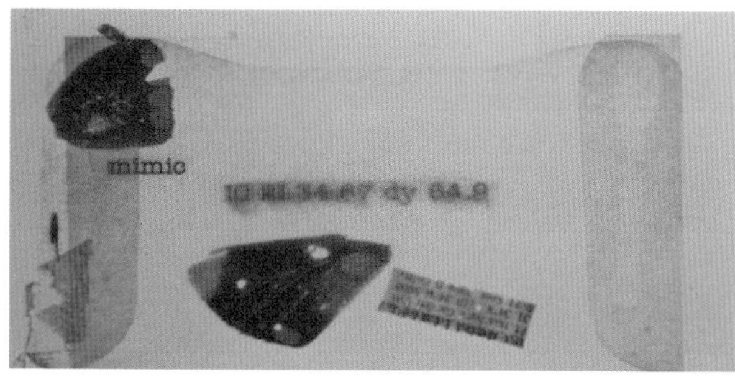
mimic

mimic

alexander goodwin
10.154.4 sf 91.

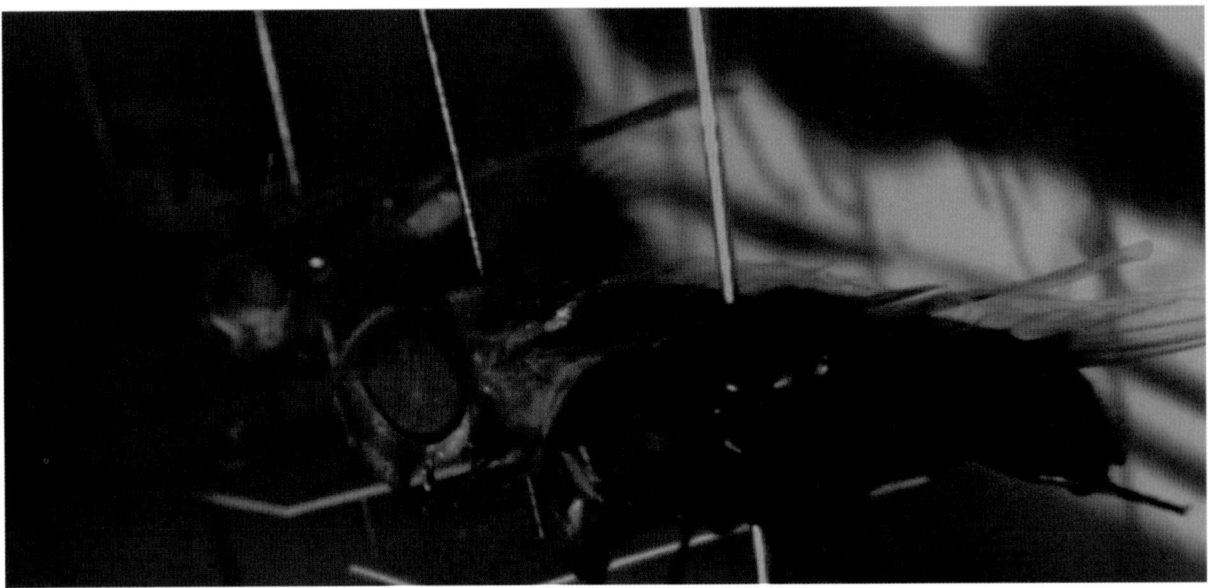

cinematic
spreads in
search

NEWS
YORK'S ETOWN N WSPAPER
Sunday, Dec 29, 1996
TOLL REACHES 1000
STRICKLER'S

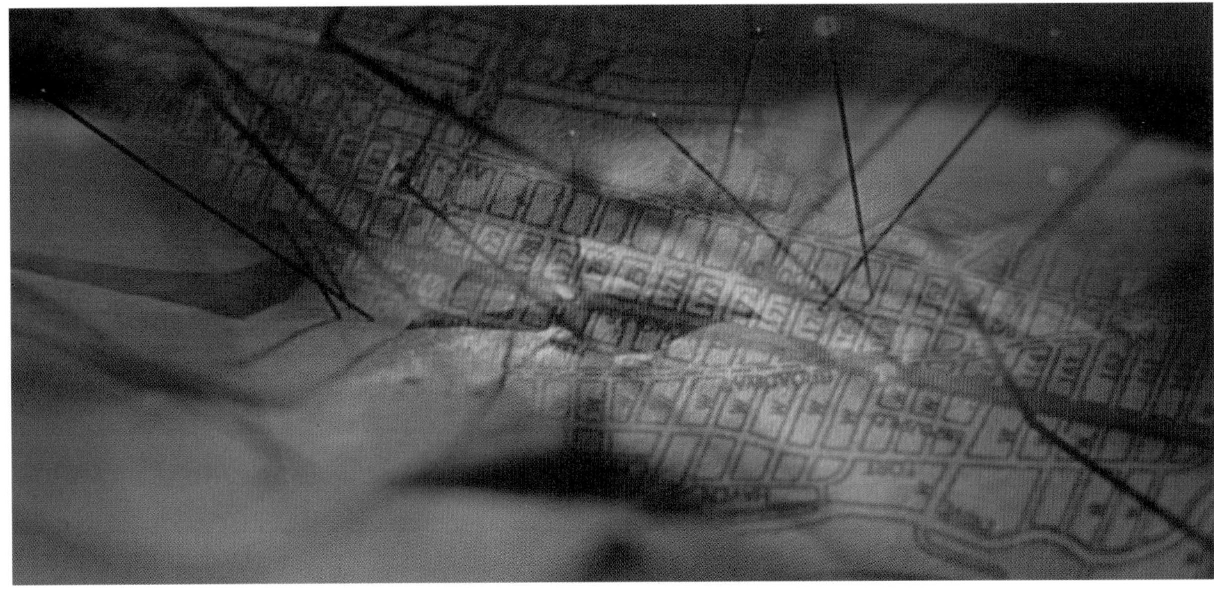

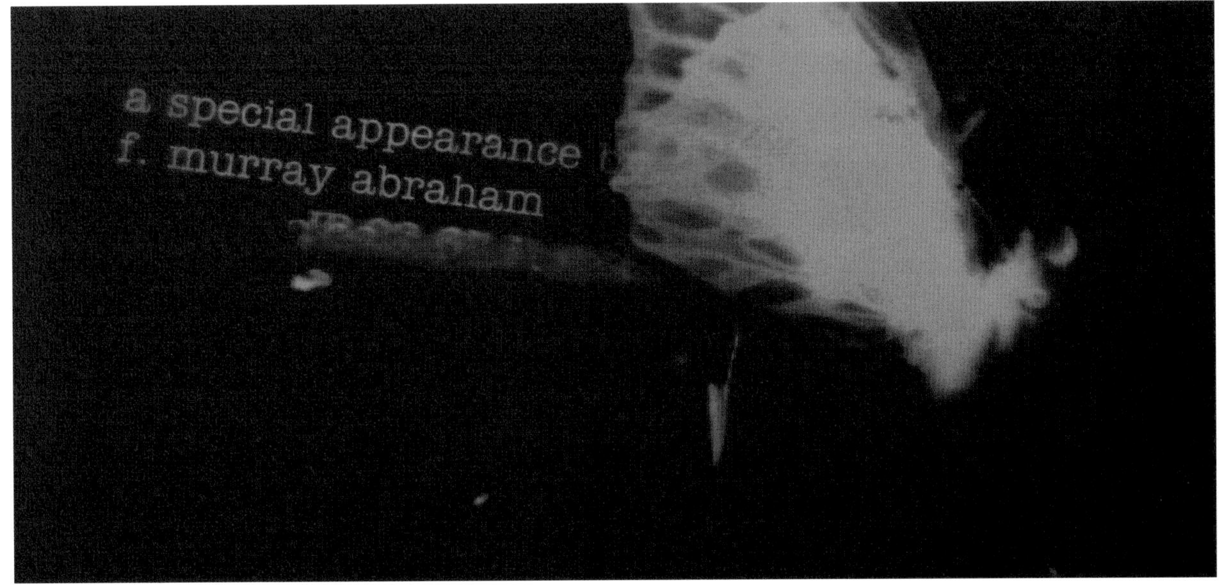
a special appearance
f. murray abraham

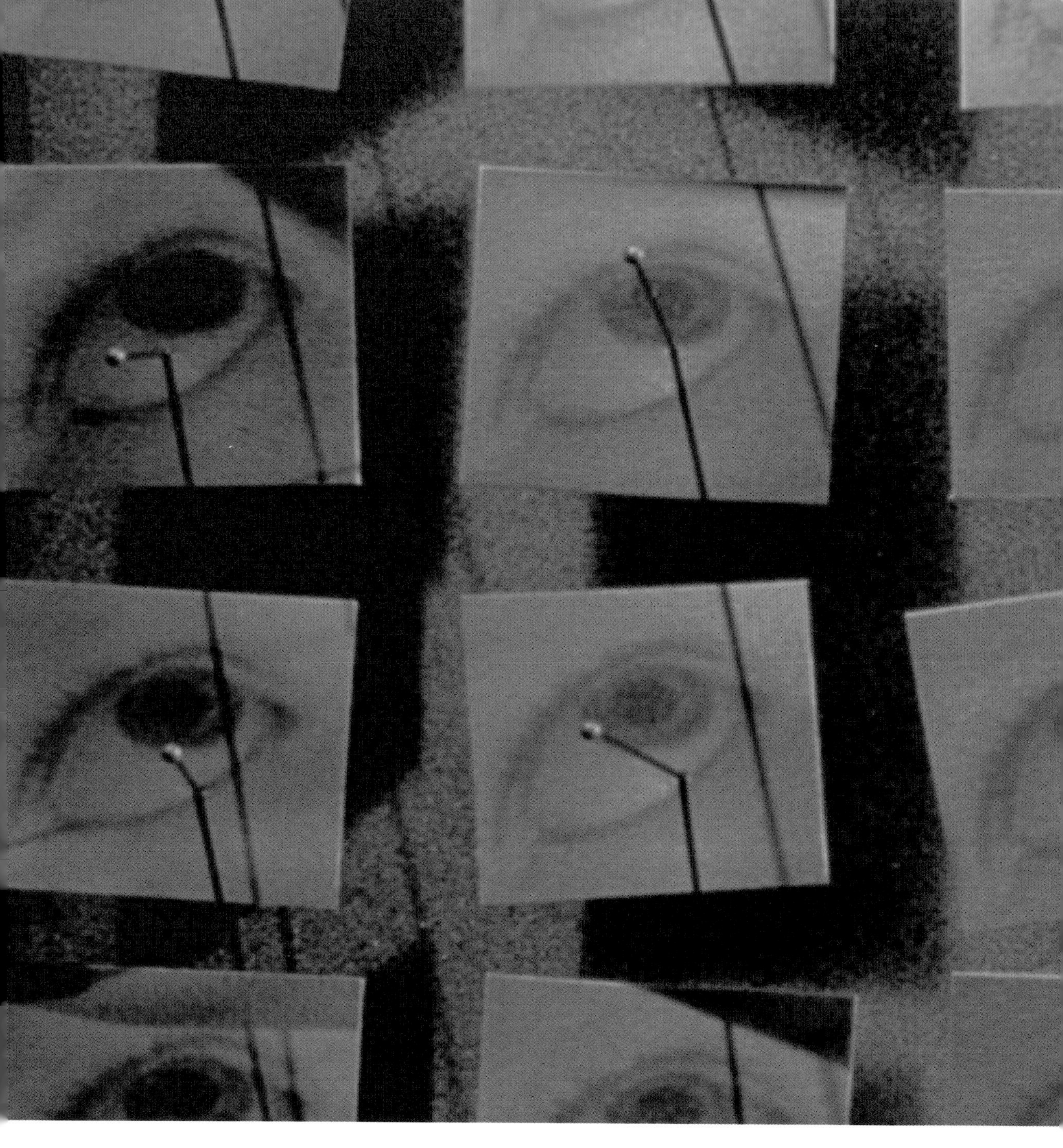

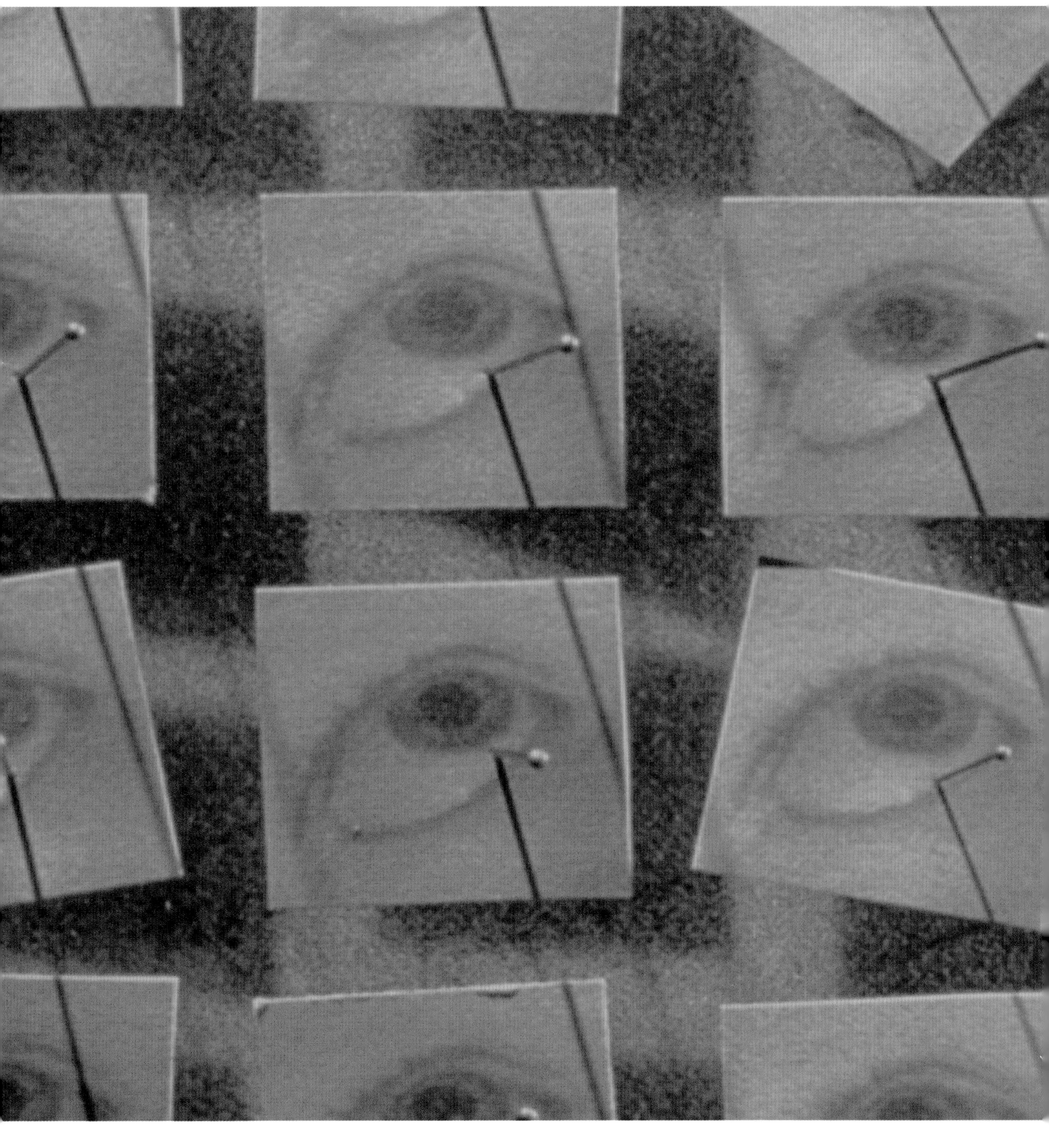

Nightwatch

Director – Ole Bornedal, 1998
Titles – Kyle Cooper (dir.)
for Imaginary Forces

Yet another story about a serial killer, *Nightwatch* provides fuel for the flame of Cooper's obsession with eyes. For this film about a serial killer whose hallmark is removing the eyeballs of his victims, Cooper scratches or cuts out the eyes on a series of photographs of young women. This approach, though simple, effectively references the reduction of human to corpse, the spirit having vacated the body in death. An added layer of distance is added by submerging the photos in water, which ripples spectrally on the screen. The type, which is projected onto the water, comes in and out of focus, layered on top of eerily glowing live-action images from the TV coverage of the most recent murder, which segues into the narrative beginning of the film.

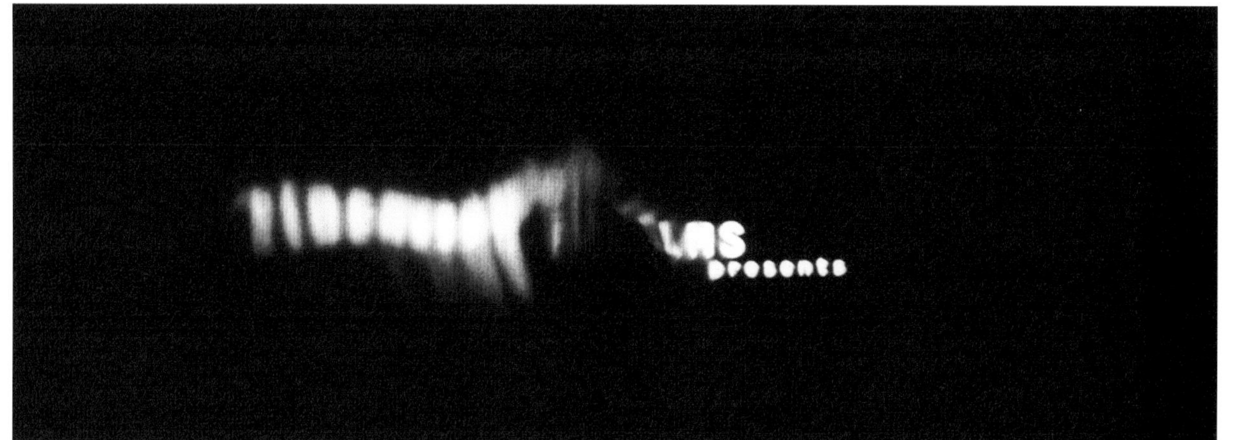

A MICHAEL OBEL
production

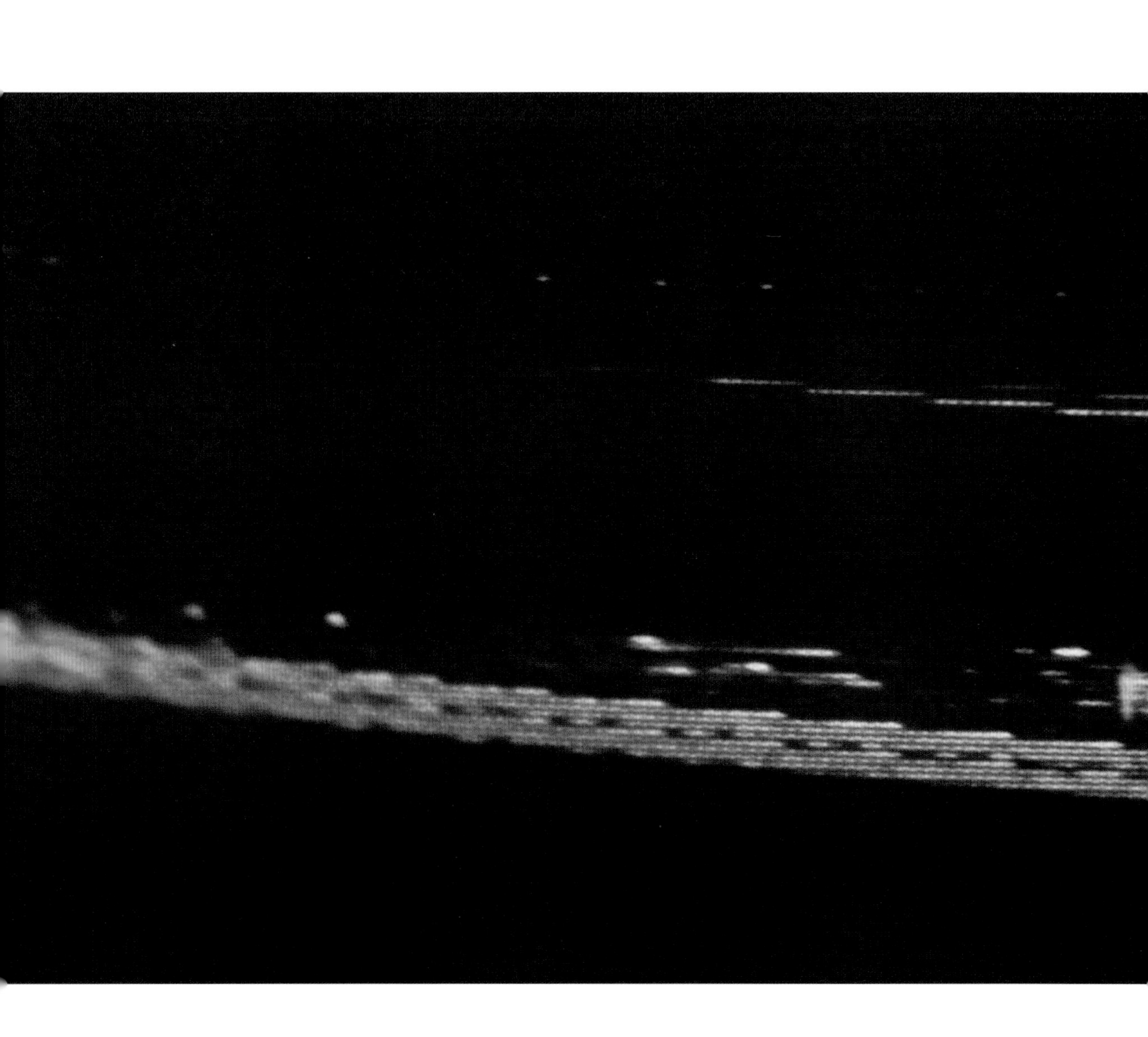

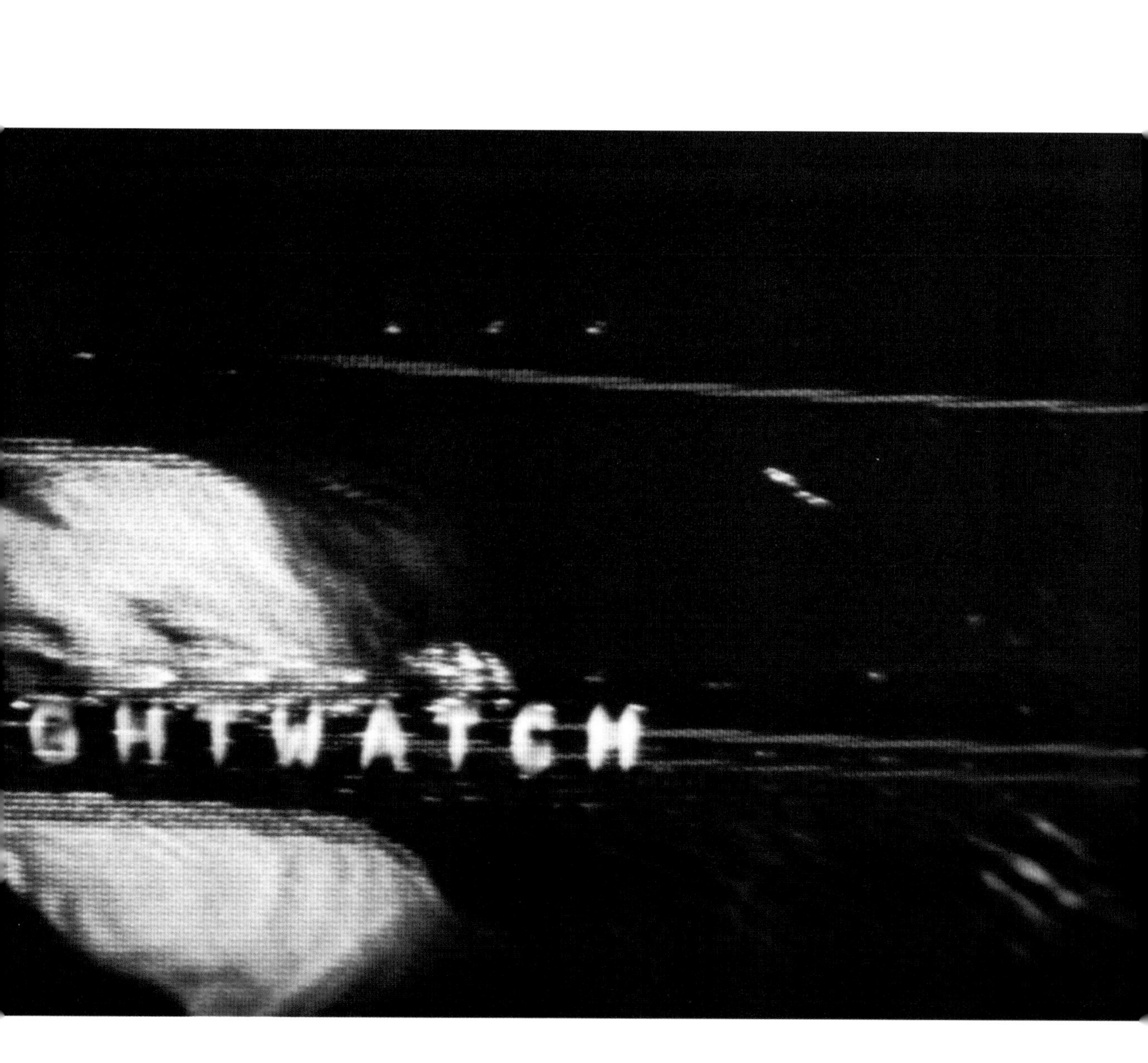
GHTWATCH

Sphere

Director – Barry Levinson, 1998
Titles – Kyle Cooper (creative dir.)
for Imaginary Forces

When first approached to create main titles for Barry Levinson's *Sphere*, one thing was clear to Cooper: "We have to have fish with teeth – evil fish." After creating idea boards containing old engravings and line drawings of sea creatures with sharp-toothed maws and shooting them through glass for a watery effect, Cooper and colleague Mikon van Gastel had the idea of actually spherizing the type itself. The result is another hallucinatory paean to the horror and suspense genre that so influenced Cooper when he was an adolescent. Sceptical of the use of high technology in the service of main titles, Cooper admits that the contrast of the slick, spherized type with hoary images of sea-monster lore provides an appropriate metaphor for the story, which in a fusion of past, present and future concerns an ancient sphere resting on the bottom of the sea that comes from the future.

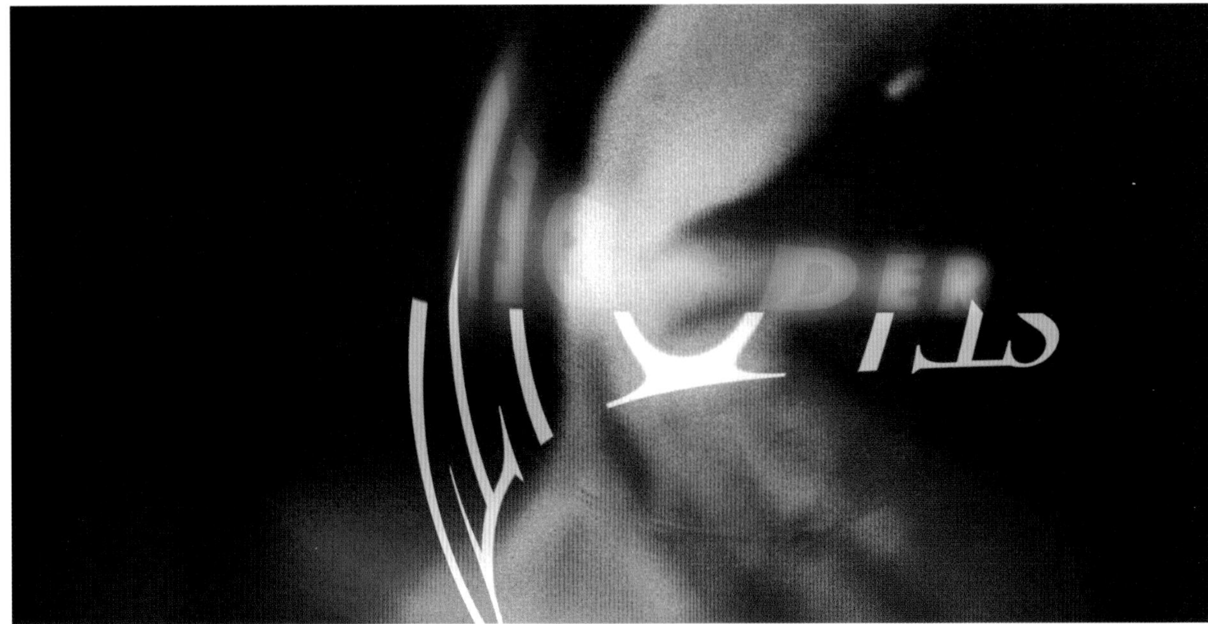

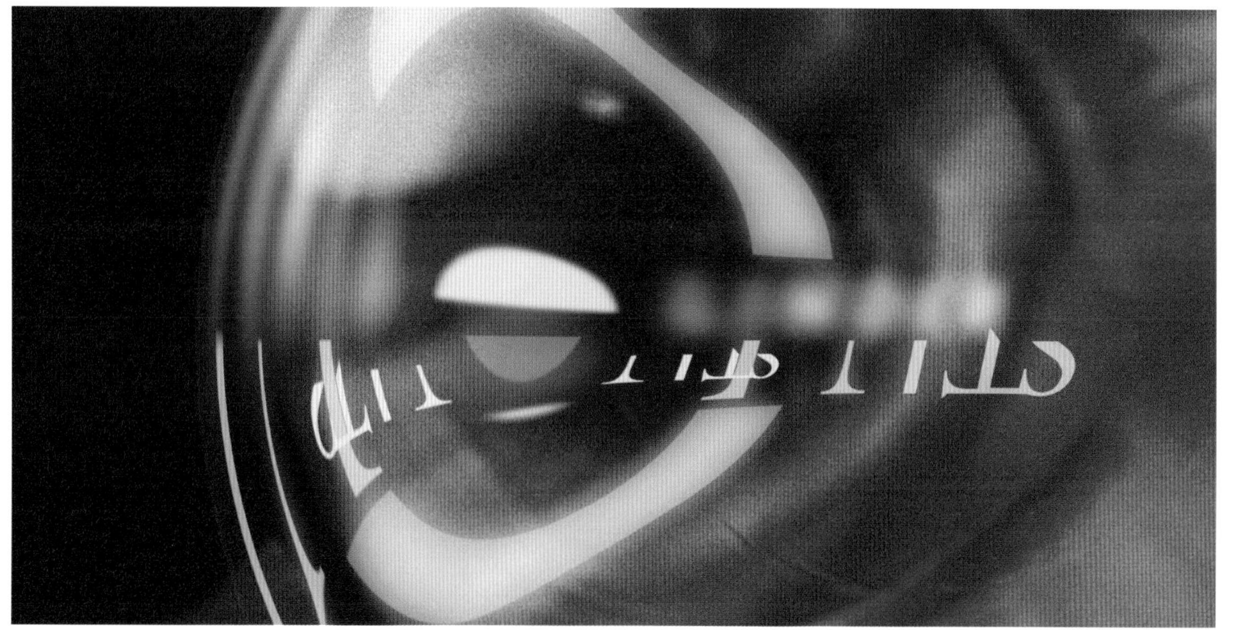

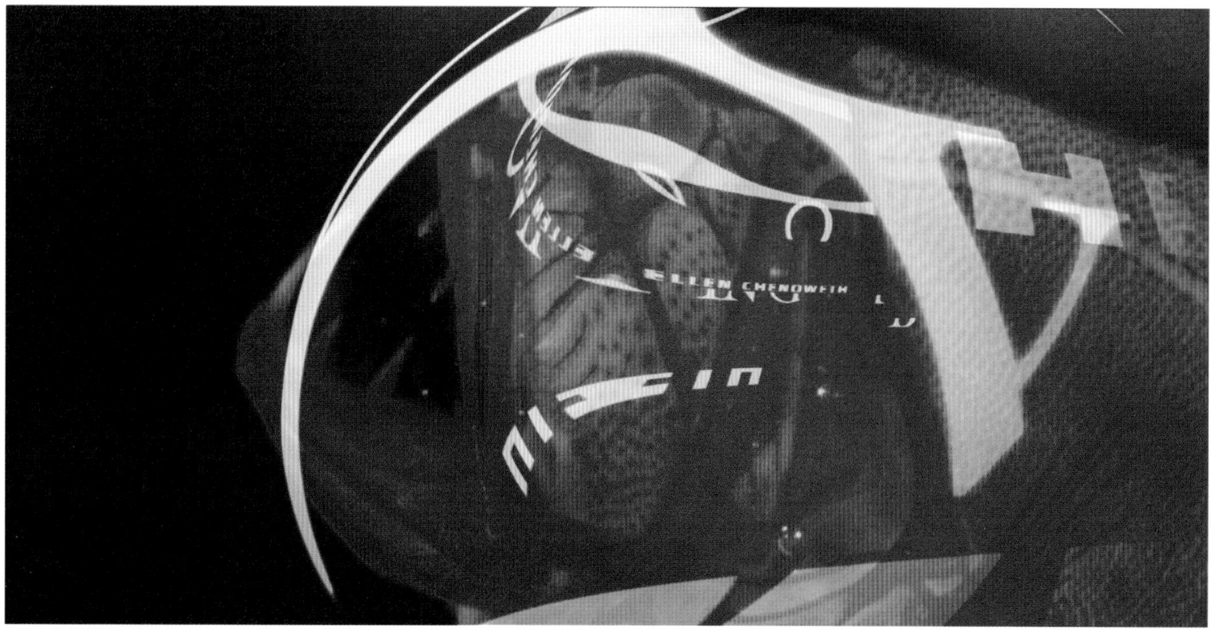

81

Arlington Road

Director – Mark Pellington, 1999
Titles – Kyle Cooper (dir.)
for Imaginary Forces

In Cooper's visual world, beauty and brutality, comfort and catastrophe are flip-sides of the same coin, as can be seen clearly in this opening sequence to Mark Pellington's *Arlington Road*, a film about the threat of domestic terrorism. In this case, the American dream of suburbia becomes a paranoid nightmare through the use of reversed-out film stock, queasy colours and a frantic sound track. Icons of the suburban idyll are foreboding in Cooper's hands: a Dalmatian chewing on a bone becomes a toothy menace; a gas meter transforms into a tool of terrorism; a toddler behind a child-protection gate looks like a prisoner of a domestic torture chamber. Cooper's own experience of suburbia, growing up outside of Boston, only serves to enhance his sense of American gothic. "Mark and I really wanted to get the sense that life in the suburbs is not safe at all," says Cooper, "that at any minute something really bad could happen."

ROBERT GOSSETT

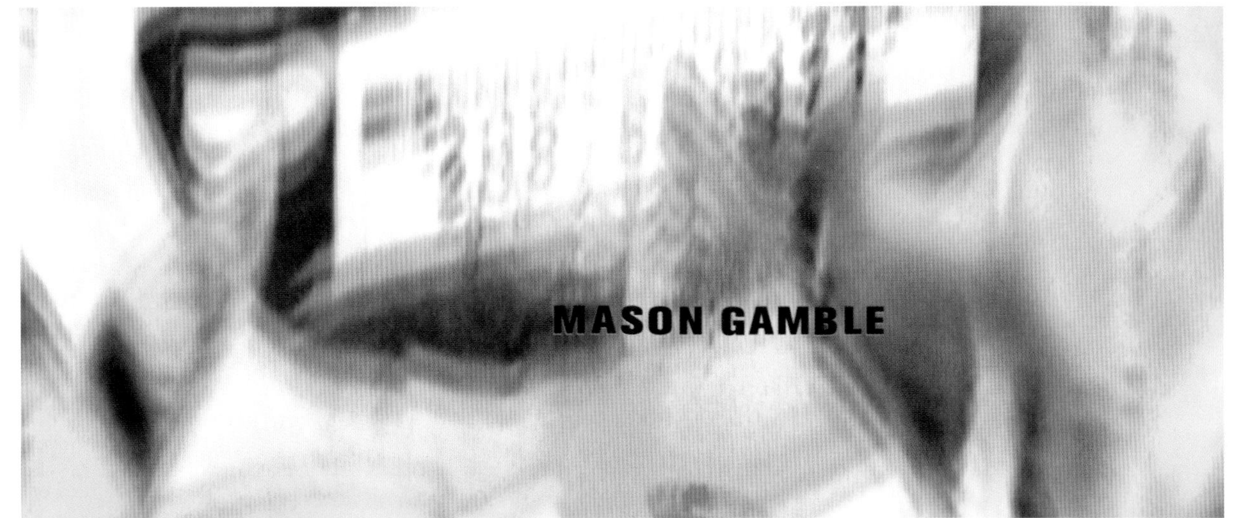
MASON GAMBLE

SPENCER TREAT CLARK

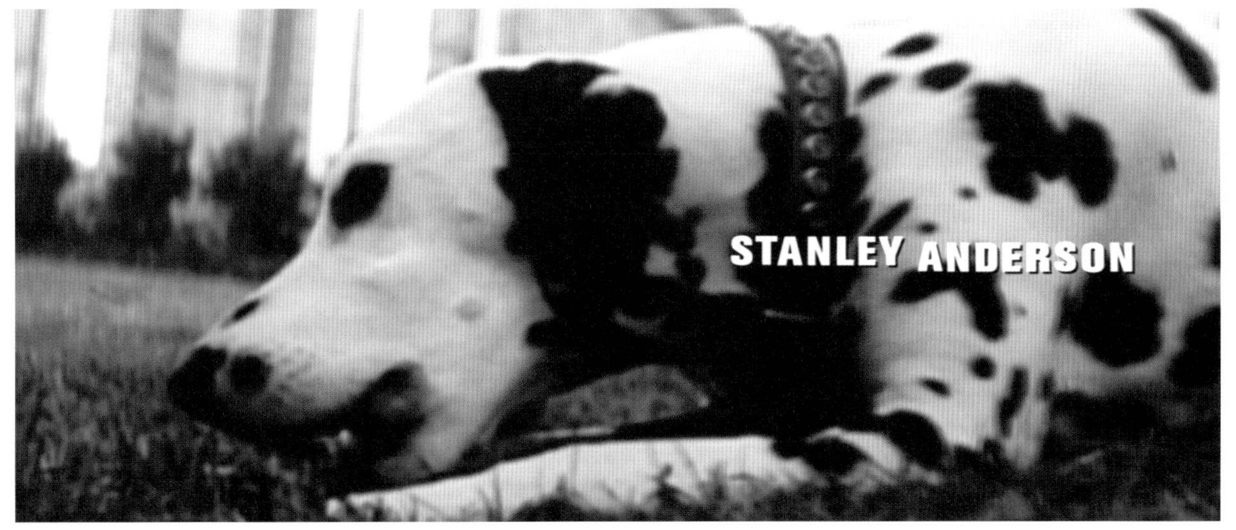
STANLEY ANDERSON

CASTING BY ELLEN CHENOWETH & KATHLEEN CHOPIN
TRACY KAPLAN

DIRECTED BY MARK PELLING

The Mummy

Director – Stephen Sommers, 1999
Titles – Kyle Cooper (dir.)
for Imaginary Forces

For the end credits of this classic tale about the living dead, Cooper and his team conducted extensive research into Egyptian culture and ancient hieroglyphs. By creating a hybrid typeface based on roman characters with serifs that incorporate hieroglyphic flourishes, Cooper manages to reference the mummy, which reanimates itself by stealing the organs and body parts of unfortunate victims. Credits appear against the backdrop of Egyptian scrolls and the secret wall inscriptions buried deep in the crypts of pyramids that were long closed to the living. In reference to the exploration of such a necropolis, a torch-reminiscent light reveals the intricate carvings and marks on the wall, and activates credits that appear horizontally and vertically as seemingly authentic hieroglyphs.

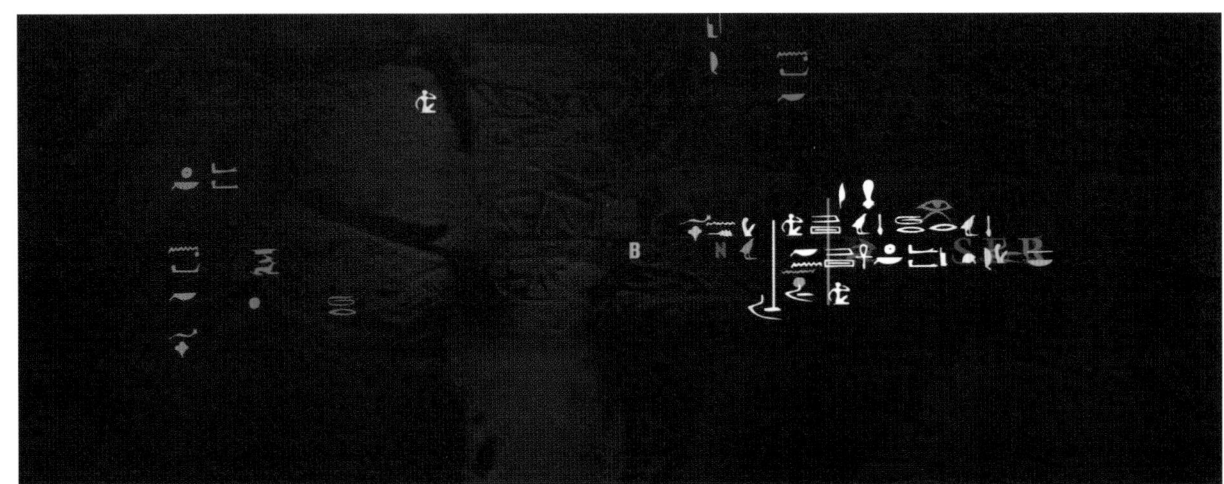

BRENDAN
FRASER

Titus

Director – Julie Taymor, 1999
Four sequences within film – Kyle Cooper (dir.) for Imaginary Forces

When director Julie Taymor decided to adapt Shakespeare's *Titus Andronicus* for the screen, she called on Cooper to create what she terms "Penny Arcade Nightmares" to be slotted into the main body of the film. Cooper's lushly dark scenarios fit in with Taymor's visual ethos, which emphasizes themes of violence, race, blood and family through sepulchral lighting, surrealistic juxtapositions and a symbolic language that runs throughout the production.
In this hallucination, the general Titus envisions revenge in the shape of a ghastly creature crowned with sharp-bladed knives. "I am Revenge," the spectre says, "sent from the infernal kingdom." Revenge lures the near-mad Titus to fight back against the character of the Goth queen Tamora, who has his daughter raped. Seated on a sculpture of a lion, the grotesque vision is flanked by creatures that are half-man, half-animal – a nod to Ovid's *Metamorphoses*, which inspired Taymor in this adaptation – and two spiralling wheels of light that add a distinctly carnivalesque atmosphere

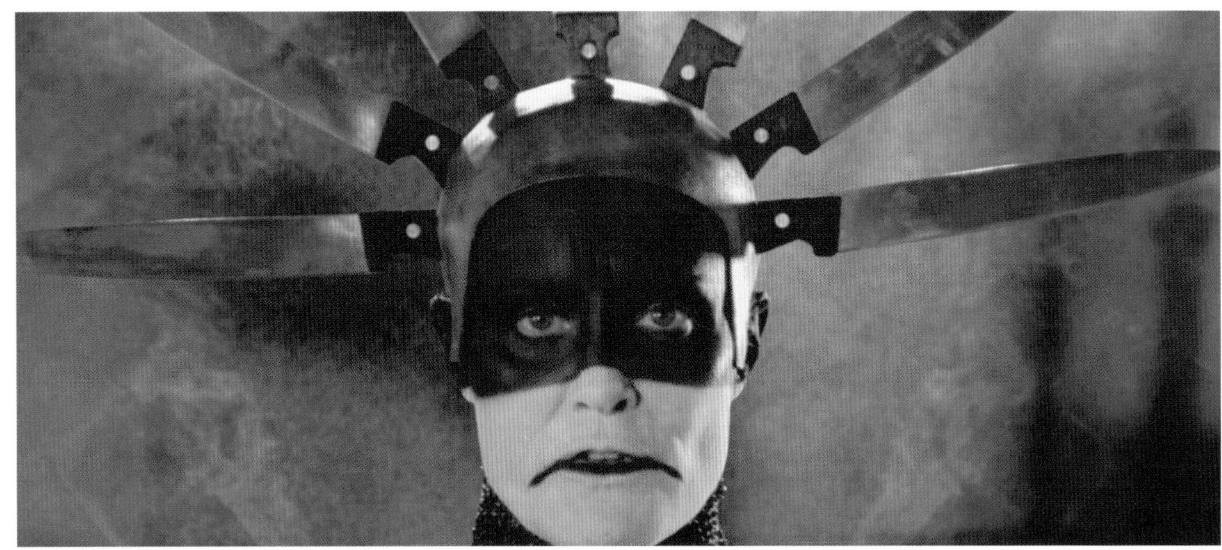

to the already hellish spectacle. Using live-action footage shot by Taymor against a blue screen and cutting in animations and lighting effects, Cooper's work punctuates this already dark rendition of Shakespeare's timeless story.

New Port South

Director – Kyle Cooper, 2001
Touchstone Pictures

Cooper took a sabbatical from Imaginary Forces for a year to direct *New Port South*, a feature film produced by teen-film legend John Hughes and written by his son James. Although the film had a very limited engagement in the Chicago area before it went to video, Cooper claims the experience was critical to his creative development. One thing Cooper was able to do was bust design out of its usual title constraints and embed it into the actual narrative. Much of the film concerns a group of students who rebel against their overly legalistic school – often through a series of graphic interventions. Guerrilla flyers, Barbara Kruger-reminiscent film sequences and silkscreen posters become vehicles for protest. Even the school's name, New Port South, becomes graphically subverted when the "S" is exchanged for a "Y".

A STUDENT
MUST BE IN

EXPECTATIONS
Expression
THE PRIMARY RESPONSIBILITY OF HIGH SCHOOL IS TO PROVIDE FOR THE
MAXIMUM LEARNING AND GROWTH
IT WILL ONLY BE INVOLVED WITH STUDENT'S
DRESS AND GROOMING AS PROVIDED
BY LAW.

expected
to treat each other with
dignity and respect

treat each other with
dignity and
attitude

WAR!

DIRECTED BY Kyle
COOPER

Spider-Man

Director – Brian De Palma, 2002
Titles – Kyle Cooper (dir.)
for Imaginary Forces

In addition to reading monster magazines, Cooper occasionally followed comic-book characters like the Incredible Hulk and the Fantastic Four when he was growing up. He even painted superhero monsters on the walls of a basement bedroom and imagined that they would jump down to rescue him if he were ever in trouble. Given this background, the opportunity to create an animated logo for Marvel Entertainment and the film titles for *Spider-Man* was no doubt appealing. By taking well-known superheroes and using them to evolve the all-cap Marvel logo, Imaginary Forces was able to have fun with the exaggerated graphic flourishes that comic books are known for. The superhero's status as battler of evil and injustice comes through in the motion graphics for *Spider-Man*, which feature the title vehicle of massive spider's webs caught between skyscrapers that capture random letters that then spell out the name of cast and crew. Like flies in a spider's sticky trap, no malfeasance will escape Spider-Man's justice.

MARVEL™

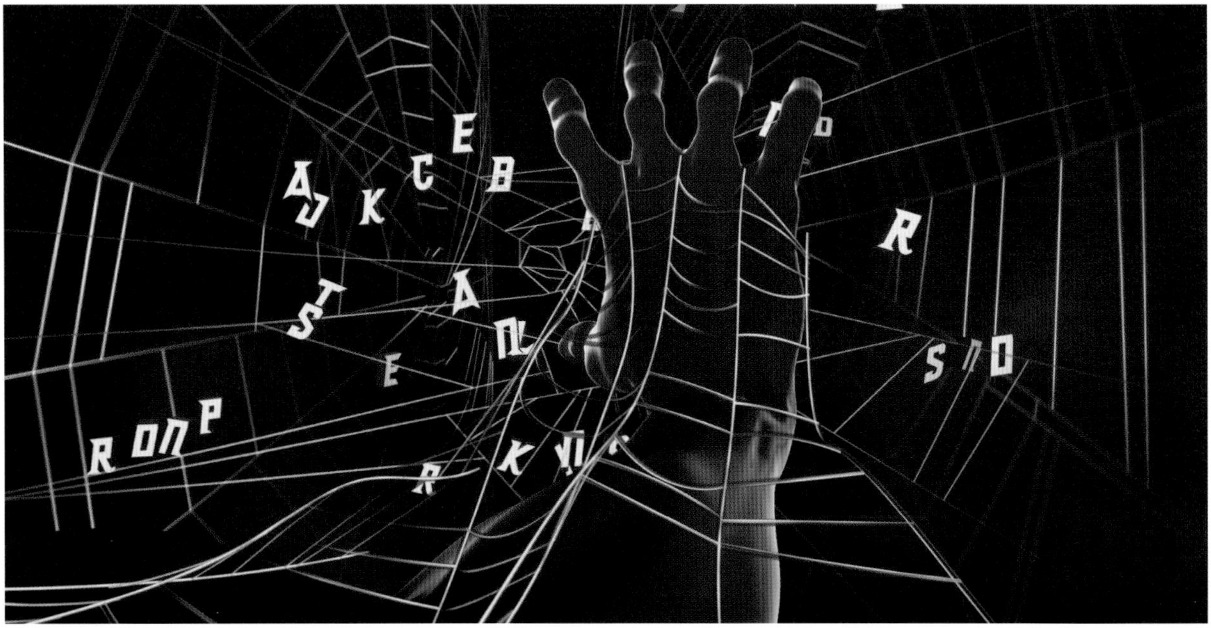

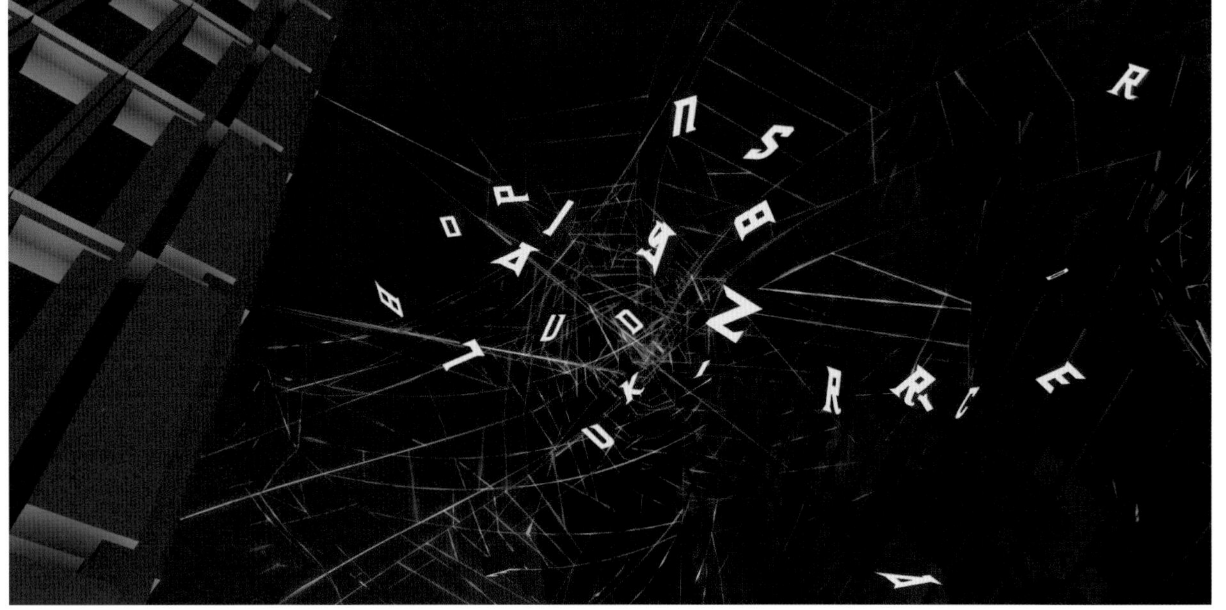

R E C T E D

BY
SAM RAIMI

Filmmaking Stamps

Art director – Kyle Cooper, 2002
Imaginary Forces

In an attempt to liven up its normally dull and pedestrian offerings, the American Postal Service has commissioned series of stamps commemorating culture and the arts in the United States. Cooper was chosen to create a behind-the-scenes look at American filmmaking, complete with 37-cent stamps lauding the work of directors, composers, cinematographers and the like. Elegiac scenes in black and white are superimposed with scribbled movie slates and edges that look like they could slot into a film projector. John Cassavetes spreads his hands out in the classic director's framing pose (Direction); Boris Karloff receives the finishing touches to his Frankenstein mask (Makeup); an anonymous hand gingerly snips two frames off a film reel (Film Editing). Tellingly, of the ten stamps that make up the series, not one hails the art of main-titles design.

USA 37
MAKEUP
BEHIND THE SCENES 06
2003
FILM EDITING
FILM MAKING
USA 37
2003
ART DIRECTION
FILM MAKING
USA 37
2003
USA 37
MUSICAL COMPOSING
FILM MAKING
2003

Dreamcatcher

Director – Lawrence Kasdan, 2003
Titles – Kyle Cooper (dir.)
for Imaginary Forces

For this film version of a Stephen King novel about aliens entering the lives of a group of friends during a winter hunting trip in Maine, Cooper created a subtly creepy sequence using nothing more than a dreamcatcher, some water and a freezer. Macro-photographic vignettes of ice crystals forming in water leave an eerie impression of morphosis. Intercut with aerial photographs of dense, wooded countryside and time-lapse images of stars moving in the sky, the overall effect is desolate and haunting. The opening's straightforward typography periodically ripples, shudders or otherwise distorts – as if in reaction to some cold wind or frisson of fear.

Dreamcatcher

Complete Projects

1988
Laserman
Dir: Peter Wang
Prod: Cooper & Yu
Designed in collaboration with Garson Yu

1989
Life Lessons (segment in *New York Stories*)
Dir: Martin Scorsese
Prod: RGA/NY
She-Devil
Dir: Susan Seidelman
Prod: RGA/NY
Designed in collaboration with Bruce Schluter

1990
Bird on a Wire
Dir: John Badham
Prod: RGA/NY
The Bonfire of the Vanities
Dir: Brian De Palma
Prod: RGA/NY
Designed in collaboration with Bruce Schluter
Home Alone
Dir: Chris Columbus
Prod: RGA/NY
Designed in collaboration with Liz Beloff
Narrow Margin
Dir: Peter Hyams
Prod: RGA/NY
Designed in collaboration with Bruce Schluter
Predator 2
Dir: Stephen Hopkins
Prod: RGA/NY
Designed in collaboration with Tom Barham

1991
Body Parts
Dir: Eric Red
Prod: RGA/NY
Curly Sue
Dir: John Hughes
Prod: RGA/NY
Designed in collaboration with Randy Akers
Don't Tell Mom the Babysitter's Dead
Dir: Stephen Herek
Prod: RGA/NY
Designed in collaboration with Brian Guidry
Frankie and Johnny
Dir: Gary Marshall
Prod: RGA/NY
Designed in collaboration with Michael Riley
The Hard Way
Dir: John Badham
Prod: RGA/NY
McBain
Dir: James Glickenhaus
Prod: RGA/NY
Men of Respect
Dir: William Reilly
Prod: RGA/NY

1992
Home Alone 2
Dir: Chris Columbus
Prod: RGA/NY
Designed in collaboration with John DiRe
Newsies
Dir: Kenny Ortega
Prod: RGA/NY
Designed in collaboration with Michael Riley
Passenger 57
Dir: Kevin Hooks
Prod: RGA/NY
Designed in collaboration with Michael Riley
Passion Fish
Dir: John Sayles
Prod: RGA/NY
Designed in collaboration with Michael Riley
Used People
Dir: Beeban Kidron
Prod: RGA/NY
Designed in collaboration with Richard Greenberg
Zebrahead
Dir: Anthony Drazen
Prod: RGA/NY
Designed in collaboration with Stacey Zabolotney

1993
The American President
Dir: Rob Reiner
Prod: RGA/NY
Body Snatchers
Dir: Abel Ferrara
Prod: RGA/NY
Designed in collaboration with Jakob Trollbeck
Carlito's Way
Dir: Brian De Palma
Prod: RGA/NY
Designed in collaboration with Michael Riley
Free Willy
Dir: Simon Wincer
Prod: RGA/NY
Designed in collaboration with Garson Yu
Indecent Proposal
Dir: Adrian Lyne
Prod: RGA/NY
Designed in collaboration with John DiRe
The Joy Luck Club
Dir: Wayne Wang
Prod: RGA/NY
Designed in collaboration with Garson Yu
Last Action Hero
Dir: John McTiernan
Prod: RGA/NY
Designed in collaboration with Richard Greenberg
Matinee
Dir: Joe Dante
Prod: RGA/NY
Designed in collaboration with Michael Riley
The Nutcracker
Dir: Emile Ardolino
Prod: RGA/NY
Designed in collaboration with Richard Greenberg
Rising Sun
Dir: Philip Kaufman
Prod: RGA/NY
Designed in collaboration with Richard Greenberg and John DiRe
Sister Act 2 (end credit sequence)
Dir: Bill Duke
Prod: RGA/NY
Designed in collaboration with Garson Yu

1994
Amos & Andrew
Dir: E. Max Frye
Prod: RGA/NY
Angels in the Outfield
Dir: William Dear
Prod: RGA/NY
The Getaway
Dir: Roger Donaldson
Prod: RGA/NY
Immortal Beloved
Dir: Bernard Rose
Prod: RGA/NY
Designed in collaboration with Garson Yu
Lipstick Camera
Dir: Mike Bonifer
Prod: RGA/NY
Designed in collaboration with Garson Yu
North
Dir: Rob Reiner
Prod: RGA/NY
Designed in collaboration with Richard Greenberg
Quiz Show (end credit montage)
Dir: Robert Redford
Prod: RGA/NY
Richie Rich
Dir: Donald Petrie
Prod: RGA/NY
True Lies
Dir: James Cameron
Prod: RGA/NY
When a Man Loves a Woman
Dir: Luis Mandoki
Prod: RGA/NY
Designed in collaboration with Garson Yu
Wolf
Dir: Mike Nichols
Prod: RGA/NY
Designed in collaboration with Richard Greeberg and Garson Yu

1995
Braveheart
Dir: Mel Gibson
Prod: RGA/NY
Dead Presidents
Dir: The Hughes Brothers
Prod: RGA/NY
Nixon
Dir: Oliver Stone
Prod: Imaginary Forces
Designed in collaboration with Michael Riley
Seven
Dir: David Fincher
Prod: RGA/NY
Designed in collaboration with David Fincher and Jenny Shainin

1996
Bio-Dome
Dir: Jason Bloom
Prod: Imaginary Forces
Designed in collaboration with Thomas Cobb and Jenny Shainin
Bogus
Dir: Norman Jewison
Prod: Imaginary Forces
Designed in collaboration with Karin Fong
Celtic Pride
Dir: Tom Decerchio
Prod: Imaginary Forces
Eraser
Dir: Charles Russell
Prod: RGA/NY
Designed in collaboration with Garson Yu
The Fan
Dir: Tony Scott
Prod: RGA/NY
Designed in collaboration with Garson Yu
Ghosts of Mississippi
Dir: Rob Reiner
Prod: Imaginary Forces
Designed in collaboration with Karin Fong
Gotti
Dir: Robert Harmon
Prod: Imaginary Forces
Designed in collaboration with Garson Yu and Olivia D'Ablis
The Island of Dr. Moreau
Dir: John Frankenheimer
Prod: RGA/LA
Designed in collaboration with Karin Fong
The Juror
Dir: Brian Gibson
Prod: RGA/LA
Designed in collaboration with Garson Yu
Mission: Impossible
Dir: Brian De Palma
Prod: RGA/LA
101 Dalmations
Dir: Stephen Herek
Prod: Imaginary Forces
Designed in collaboration with Garson Yu
Twister
Dir: Jan De Bont
Prod: Imaginary Forces
Designed in collaboration with Garson Yu
White Squall
Dir: Ridley Scott
Prod: Imaginary Forces
Designed in collaboration with Garson Yu

1997
Donnie Brasco
Dir: Mike Newell
Prod: Imaginary Forces
Designed in collaboration with Kurt Mattila and Olivia D'Ablis
Flubber
Dir: Les Mayfield
Prod: Imaginary Forces
Designed in collaboration with Michael Riley and Grant Lau

George Wallace
Dir: John Frankenheimer
Prod: Imaginary Forces
Designed in collaboration with Michael Riley and Olivia D'Ablis
Limbo
Dir: John Sayles
Prod: Imaginary Forces
Designed in collaboration with Michael Riley
Men with Guns
Dir: John Sayles
Prod: Imaginary Forces
Designed in collaboration with Michael Riley and Eric Smith
Metro
Dir: Thomas Carter
Prod: Imaginary Forces
Mimic
Dir: Guillermo Del Toro
Prod: Imaginary Forces
Designed in collaboration with Karin Fong, Kimberly Cooper and Dana Yee
Mouse Hunt
Dir: Gore Verbinski
Prod: Imaginary Forces
Designed in collaboration with Michael Riley
Nunzio's Second Cousin
Dir: Tom DeCherchio
Prod: Imaginary Forces
Designed in collaboration with Garson Yu
Red Corner
Dir: Jon Avnet
Prod: Imaginary Forces
Designed in collaboration with Jennifer Chang
Volcano
Dir: Mick Jackson
Prod: Imaginary Forces
Designed in collaboration with Garson Yu

1998

The Avengers
Dir: Jeremiah Chechik
Prod: Imaginary Forces
Designed in collaboration with Karin Fong and Mikon Van Gastel
City of Angels
Dir: Brad Silberling
Prod: Imaginary Forces
Designed in collaboration with Adam Bluming
Fallen
Dir: Gregory Hoblitt
Prod: Imaginary Forces
Designed in collaboration with Scarlet Kim
The Horse Whisperer
Dir: Robert Redford
Prod: Imaginary Forces
Jack Frost
Dir: Troy Miller
Prod: Imaginary Forces
Lost in Space
Dir: Stephen Hopkins
Prod: Imaginary Forces
Designed in collaboration with Mikon Van Gastel
Mask of Zorro
Dir: Martin Campbell
Prod: Imaginary Forces
Designed in collaboration with Michael Riley
Mighty Joe Young
(sequence not used)
Dir: Ron Underwood
Prod: Imaginary Forces
The Negotiator
Dir: F. Gary Gray
Prod: Imaginary Forces
Designed in collaboration with Olivia D'Ablis and Mike Jakab
Nightwatch
Dir: Ole Bornedal
Prod: Imaginary Forces
Designed in collaboration with Kimberly Cooper and Michelle Doherty
The Parent Trap
Dir: Nancy Meyers
Prod: Imaginary Forces
Designed in collaboration with Michelle Doherty
The Rat Pack (main title and montages)
Dir: Rob Cohen
Prod: Imaginary Forces
Designed in collaboration with Kimberly Cooper
Sphere
Dir: Barry Levinson
Prod: Imaginary Forces
Designed in collaboration with Mikon Van Gastel, Kurt Mattila, Olivia D'Ablis and Michael Riley
Without Limits
Dir: Robert Towne
Prod: Imaginary Forces
Designed in collaboration with Dana Yee

1999

Arlington Road
Dir: Mark Pellington
Prod: Imaginary Forces
The General's Daughter
Dir: Simon West
Prod: Imaginary Forces
Designed in collaboration with Michelle Doherty
The Mummy
Dir: Stephen Sommers
Prod: Imaginary Forces
Designed in collaboration with Mike Jakab and Eric Cruz
Pushing Tin
Dir: Mike Newell
Prod: Imaginary Forces
The Story of Us
Dir: Rob Reiner
Prod: Imaginary Forces
Designed in collaboration with Rapheal Macho
Three Kings
Dir: David O. Russell
Prod: Imaginary Forces
Titus
(nightmare sequences)
Dir: Julie Taymor
Prod: Imaginary Forces
Designed in collaboration with Michelle Doherty
Wild Wild West
Dir: Barry Sonnenfeld
Prod: Imaginary Forces

2000

The Crossing
Dir: Robert Harmon
Prod: Imaginary Forces
Designed in collaboration with Rapheal Macho
The Mummy Returns
Dir: Stephen Sommers
Prod: Imaginary Forces
Designed in collaboration with Charles Khoury and Mike Jakab
Reindeer Games
(sequence not used)
Dir: John Frankenheimer
Prod: Imaginary Forces

2001

K-Pax
Directed by Iain Softley
Prod: Imaginary Forces
Designed in collaboration with Michelle Doherty
New Port South
Dir: Kyle Cooper
Studio: Touchstone Pictures and John Hughes production

2002

Filmmaking Stamps
Created in collaboration with Kimberly Cooper, Ethel Kessler and Jennifer Gallo
Metal Gear Solid 2
Dir: Hideo Kojima
Prod: Imaginary Forces
Created in collaboration with Ellery Gave
Path to War
Dir: John Frankenheimer
Prod: Imaginary Forces
Spider-Man
Dir: Sam Raimi
Prod: Imaginary Forces
Designed in collaboration with Charles Khoury and Ahmet Ahmet

2003

Darkness Falls
(prologue and main and end credit sequence)
Dir: Jonathan Liebesman
Prod: Imaginary Forces
Designed in collaboration with Brian Mah and Ahmet Ahmet
Dreamcatcher
Dir: Lawrence Kasdan
Prod: Imaginary Forces
Designed in collaboration with Bradley Grolsh and Charles Khoury
Identity
Dir: James Mangold
Prod: Imaginary Forces

Notes, Selected Bibliography, and Credits

Notes

1. Kimberly Cooper, interview, 16 February 2001.

2. In what must have seemed like a dream come true, *Fangoria* ran an article about Cooper's work: Michael Gingold, "Title Frights", *Fangoria*, no. 160, 1996, pp. 52–3.

3. Unless otherwise indicated, all Cooper quotations come from interviews with the author held on 15–16 February 2001, or from telephone conversations over the course of a year.

4. Beatrice Ward, "The Crystal Goblet", *Looking Closer 3: Classic Writings on Graphic Design*, New York: Allworth Press, 1999, p. 56.

5. Angela Aleiss, "The Names behind the Titles", *Variety*, 8–14 December 1997, p. 86.

6. Janet Abrams, "Eye Openers", *I.D.*, November 1996, pp. 76–9.

7. Anthony Lane, "Blood Buddies", *New Yorker*, 17 March 1997, pp. 121–3.

8. Ibid., p. 121

9. Janet Maslin, "True Story, Dipping into the Classics", *New York Times*, 20 December 1996.

10. Peter Frankfurt, interview, 16 February 2001.

Selected Bibliography

Abrams, Janet, "Eye Openers", *I.D.*, November 1996, pp. 76–9.

Benenson, Laurie Halpern, "The New Look in Film Titles: Edgy Type That's on the Move", *New York Times*, 24 March 1996, Section 2, p. 22.

Caro, Mark, "Title Wave", *Chicago Tribune*, 10 December 1995, Section 7, pp. 1, 20.

Coupland, Ken, "Imaginary Forces: Taking All the Credit", *Graphis*, vol. 54, no. 312, September/October 1998, pp. 66–73.

Croal, N'Gai, "Where Credits Are Due", *Newsweek*, 10 November 1997, p. 92.

Edgar, Ray, "Micro Film", *World Art*, no. 18, 1998, pp. 24–9.

Eeuwens, Adam, "Forces to Reckon With", *Creativity*, October 1998, pp. 26–9.

"The 100 Most Creative People in Entertainment", *Entertainment*, 27 June/ 4 July 1997.

"100 Years of Stuff: Some Experts Pick the Century's Greatest Design Hits", *New York Times Magazine*, 13 December 1998, p. 65.

"Kyle Cooper: Title Card, Artist", *Millimeter*, August 1996, p. 33.

Mamera, Jeff, and Philip Zabriskie, "Anxiety Driven", *Icon Thoughtstyle Magazine*, April 1997, p. 28.

Nickell, Joe, "The Art of the Prelude", *Res*, winter 1998, pp. 14–19.

Ogundehin, Michelle, "Masterpiece of Dementia", *Blueprint*, March 1996, p. 20.

Puig, Claudia, "Making 'Seven' Audience Snap to Attention", *Los Angeles Times*, 3 November 1995, p. F8.

Surowiecki, James, "Title Wave", *Details*, March 1998, pp. 212–14.

Twemlow, Alice, "Imaginary Forces", *Graphics International*, November 1997, pp. 32–3.

Williams, David E., "Initial Images", *American Cinematographer*, May 1998, pp. 92–5.

Zappaterra, Yolanda, "Full Force", *Design Week*, vol. 16, no. 17, 26 April 2001, pp. 16–17, 19.

———, "First Impression", *Design Week*, 9 May 1997, pp. 16–17.

Credits

The publishers would like to thank Tim Nicholson of Dalton Nicholson Associates for his expert assistance in obtaining permission to illustrate works, and Kyle Cooper and all at Imaginary Forces. Kyle Cooper (kyle.kylecooper.com) would like to thank his wife, Kimberly, for her constant support and Phyllis Weisband and Rebecca Hertz for their tireless efforts in helping to get this book produced.